PRAISE FOR

## *Keeping a Piece of Her*

"A true tale of courage, faith, love, and perseverance, written with style and grace, wit and wisdom. The story will make you laugh and make you cry. Mostly it will make you feel the power of love and give you a taste of the spirit and tenacity of the characters within. Though a work of non-fiction, it reads like the best of well-crafted novels: you will come to care and feel for the characters, and miss them when the book ends. Hopefully, you will also arrive at a better understanding of what it means to love all people and, for many of us, will add to the meaning of God in our lives. Bob's work is a treasure for the soul."

—**MARIA JUAREZ**, retired NYC publishing executive

"A poignant story of bodies and souls connected through a rare gift of familial love, told with grace, warmth, and delicious wit."

—**SARA JENKINS**, author of *This Side of Nirvana*

"This book provides a meaningful look into the life of a transplant patient. As a nephrologist, it is refreshing and rewarding to see how impactful a kidney transplant can be."

—**WILLIAM DURHAM**, MD, nephrologist, Mountain Kidney and Hypertension, board certified in nephrology

"This book weaves two stories into one: part detective tale that begins with a routine urine test and part triumph over a near-fatal kidney disease, seasoned with love from family and friends. Beautifully written, with humor and sadness, Gance captures human resilience at its finest."

—**MARILYN LAKEN**, PhD, RN, author of *I've Never Been Old Before: A Practical Guide to Aging*

"In *Keeping a Piece of Her*, the author takes us on a gradually unfolding, life-threatening journey that proves a major point about healthcare crises. Know how to gather your team and learn how to ask for what you need. His story will benefit not only anyone experiencing a crisis but also anyone who has someone they love in crisis. Healthcare professionals will also see the benefit of their clear, honest, and genuine communication and care.

"This is a story told with vulnerability and wit. It will leave you with many bits of hard-earned wisdom as well as a more vibrant view of our connectedness within this human family."

—MARY E. SELBY, retired post-op nurse

"Bob Gance's *Keeping a Piece of Her* is a compelling book. It is a memoir of Bob's own medical crisis (a hereditary kidney disorder that predictably led to complete failure) and his persistence in the face of this diagnosis and the limitations it placed on him, including a dedication to distance running that made him a medal-winner.

"More importantly, and movingly, it details the gift he received from his younger sister, Rita, who unselfishly donated one of her kidneys, keeping him alive without the rigors of daily dialysis, and the sad sequel, Rita's death from ovarian cancer.

"Most of all, this book is a love story—Rita's altruistic love for her brother and his love for her, love between parents and children, husbands, wives, and life partners. It has wrenching moments and moments of fun and hilarity. The final effect is a heart-warming affirmation of human goodness."

—MERRITT MOSELEY, emeritus professor of English, University of North Carolina at Asheville, author of seven books about contemporary British fiction, most recently *A History of the Booker Prize: Contemporary Fiction Since 1992*, published London: Routledge, 2021

"This is a moving story of love and courage that details the lifesaving gift of a kidney from sister to brother. Full of anecdotes, wry humor, and deep feeling, the story reveals what it's like to donate and to receive a kidney and the immense gratitude such a gift engenders. It is not only enlightening but inspiring to read this well-crafted, lovingly immersive account."

—**JIM MCGLINN**, EdD, professor emeritus, UNC Asheville

"Bob Gance's memoir, *Keeping a Piece of Her*, is a moving and inspirational story of love, courage, and acceptance. On the surface, a reader might expect to learn about kidney disease and a successful organ transplant. Here, the deeper message is how sacrifice and love unites a brother and sister and permeates their close-knit family. It is also love that leads to the celebration of differences in identity and more than acceptance—celebration—of the unique relationship of two women. You will be moved to tears, but you will also be inspired."

—**JEANNE MCGLINN**, professor emeritus, UNC Asheville

"*Keeping a Piece of Her* is a readable and compelling retrospective on the author's battle with kidney failure and his unique relationship with his sister, his organ donor. Full of insights, humor, honesty, and selfawareness, it is a gift that will move and inspire not only patients and their families but a much broader audience."

—**ROBERT WHITE**, retired professor of English

*Keeping a Piece of Her: The Joys and Sorrows of My Second Life*

by Bob Gance

© Copyright 2025 Bob Gance

ISBN 979-8-88824-780-8

All rights reserved. No part of this publication may be reproduced, stored in a retrieval system, or transmitted in any form or by any means—electronic, mechanical, photocopy, recording, or any other—except for brief quotations in printed reviews, without the prior written permission of the author.

Cover art and design by Lauren Sheldon

Published by

◤ köehlerbooks™

3705 Shore Drive
Virginia Beach, VA 23455
800-435-4811
www.koehlerbooks.com

# KEEPING A PIECE OF HER

The Joys and Sorrows of My Second Life

## BOB GANCE

VIRGINIA BEACH
CAPE CHARLES

# TABLE OF CONTENTS

*Prologue* . . . . . . . . . . . . . . . . . . . . . . . . . . . . . . . . . . . . . . . . ix

## PART I   1

Chapter One: June 1964 . . . . . . . . . . . . . . . . . . . . . . . . . . . *3*
Chapter Two: Making the Team . . . . . . . . . . . . . . . . . . . . . 7
Chapter Three: Out the Window . . . . . . . . . . . . . . . . . . . . 15
Chapter Four: A Kick in the Gut . . . . . . . . . . . . . . . . . . . . 18
Chapter Five: The New York City Marathon . . . . . . . . . . . . . . 24
Chapter Six: Hard Pills to Swallow. . . . . . . . . . . . . . . . . . . 38
Chapter Seven: Our Dream Home . . . and Dialysis. . . . . . . . . . 45

## PART II   57

Chapter Eight: My Second Life . . . . . . . . . . . . . . . . . . . . . 59
Chapter Nine: The Best of Times, the Worst of Times . . . . . . . . 63
Chapter Ten: "I Have Finished the Race" . . . . . . . . . . . . . . . 70
Chapter Eleven: Another God Moment . . . . . . . . . . . . . . . . 78
Chapter Twelve: The Letter . . . . . . . . . . . . . . . . . . . . . . . 83
Chapter Thirteen: Good Summer. . . . . . . . . . . . . . . . . . . . 88
Chapter Fourteen: Ireland . . . . . . . . . . . . . . . . . . . . . . . . 100
Chapter Fifteen: My Body Is Torn . . . . . . . . . . . . . . . . . . . 112
Chapter Sixteen: In the Arms of the Angel . . . . . . . . . . . . . . 116

*Postscripts*. . . . . . . . . . . . . . . . . . . . . . . . . . . . . . . . . . . 123
*Epilogue* . . . . . . . . . . . . . . . . . . . . . . . . . . . . . . . . . . . . 127
*Acknowledgments* . . . . . . . . . . . . . . . . . . . . . . . . . . . . . . 132

## PROLOGUE

I had expected at least a fanfare, perhaps even a symphony. Instead, my first moment of awareness as I awoke from anesthesia took the form of a silent, bemused query. Does everyone regaining consciousness in a recovery room behold the exact same sight . . . retractable curtains on tracks? I had imagined the introduction to the new world awaiting me after my kidney transplant would have somehow been more momentous.

In what seemed like a few seconds, I sensed a comfortable warmth as though I was smothered in God's loving embrace. Either that, or someone had tucked a heated blanket around me. I slowly became aware that I was under the watchful gaze of a nurse to the right of my bed.

"Hi," I managed. She smiled warmly and pointed across the sheets to something below me and to the left. I raised my head and looked down. There, nestled securely on a tray attached below the bed, was a catheter bag almost full of pink-tinged urine and, emanating from it, a line of tubing that I realized in short order was attached to my lower parts. I turned to the nurse.

"Did that urine come from *me*?" I asked incredulously.

"Yes." She smiled. I had spent the last six and a half months on dialysis because of kidney failure brought on by Alport syndrome, the hereditary genetic anomaly that my brother Ed and I inherited from my mother. During that time, my total urine output hadn't exceeded half a gallon. I had been told that transplanted kidneys don't necessarily function immediately because of something called Delayed Graft Function. I might not see an increase in urine output immediately. But in my case, my new kidney was firing on all cylinders right off the bat.

Then the nurse pointed back over her right shoulder. "Your sister is over there."

Rita was eight years younger than me. Daughters of women with Alport are spared. When I first told her almost seven years earlier that my kidneys would eventually fail, she responded without batting an eye, "You can have one of mine." I looked over at her and waved exuberantly, pointing toward the nearly full catheter bag.

Even at the tender age of thirty-four, Reet had experienced more than her share of major surgeries, including a laminectomy (herniated disc removal) for a work-related back injury at age twenty-three and knee and shoulder procedures for various sports-related maladies. There would be more to come. She had a history of not doing well with general anesthesia, which would inevitably bring on severe nausea and vomiting postoperatively.

Open nephrectomy (kidney removal) was the standard technique for procuring a living-donor kidney at the time. When I later saw her scar, it looked as though she had been sawed in half by a magician who decided to stop two-thirds of the way through. Thirty-three staples were required to close the incision. In addition, removal of the kidney involved stretching of the lower aspect of the rib cage to allow access to the organ, resulting in pain from muscles and tendons that, to say the least, were not designed or positioned to be manipulated in that way. She would have post-op pain for months. The recipient, especially one without much abdominal fat, has a far easier time of it. Transplanted kidneys are placed anteriorly (in the front) of the lower abdomen and tucked into the pelvic recess, where they are readily hooked up to a vein, an artery, and a ureter without significant tissue trauma.

Through the pain and fog of anesthesia, she waved at me weakly, managed a tepid smile, and plopped her head back down on the pillow. Our interchange-in-mime would later become the source of a humorous anecdote, but for the time being, she felt like hell.

I spent about an hour in recovery before being transported back to my room, where my wife, JoAnne, and my mother, who had flown up from Florida, were waiting. I decided to put on a show and clasped my hands together above my head, waving them back and forth as though I had just won the Olympic Marathon. To be sure, my unexpected energy was fueled by IV prednisone coursing through my body at the rate of 100 mg per twenty-four hours. I was wheeled into my room and transferred to a bed. JoAnne kissed me on the forehead and asked how I was feeling.

"I'm horny," I replied.

"*Really?*" she exclaimed in disbelief.

"God no," I said and sank back into the pillow. Intimacy was the farthest thing from my mind, especially with a foley catheter in place to interfere with proceedings. It wasn't exactly at the top of her list either.

Throughout the afternoon, as nurses and resident physicians popped in to check on me, reality began to set in. The day my family, Rita, and I had anticipated for almost seven years had arrived. From my window, I could see the impressive Philadelphia skyline set against the backdrop of a deep blue late winter sky, a visual metaphor that spoke of the possibilities that now lie before me. It was February 20, 1990 . . . the first day of my second life.

# PART I

## CHAPTER ONE

## *June 1964*

I had expected that it would be a routine physical. At the end of my high school sophomore year, I had secured a summer job as a counselor at a day camp and would be paid the princely sum of twenty-five dollars for the summer's work. A physical was required. It was almost complete when the doctor decided I should have a litmus-stick urine screening. I dutifully peed across the sliver of paper that had a colored band on the "business end," thinking how silly this seemed. The doctor held my newly christened litmus stick next to the jar in which it had resided. The label displayed a variety of litmus screening outcomes. A concerned look spread across her face.

Then she said to my dad, "He has red blood cells in his urine."

They began an exchange to which I was oblivious because I had promptly fainted. I recovered as they knelt over me and the doctor held smelling salts under my nose. My fainting prompted a concern that I might be anemic. I was sent for blood work, bewildered, but exclaimed to my dad, "I feel fine!" My immediate fear was that I would not be able to take advantage of the dream summer job for a sixteen-year-old boy. That opportunity meant a lot to me for many reasons. My anticipated financial windfall wasn't necessarily foremost.

Two years earlier, my parents, younger siblings Ed and Rita, and I had moved from a one-bedroom apartment in Astoria, Queens, New

York, to a four-bedroom Cape Cod-style home with a half-acre yard in Commack, Long Island. I wasn't happy about the move. I had left the only home I'd known, including friends, lots of cousins, and the social structure with which I was familiar. My first day as a freshman at Commack High School was difficult, almost traumatic. I had spent the first eight years of my academic life as a student at Immaculate Conception parochial school under the watchful, protective eyes of the Sisters of the Holy Union of the Sacred Heart.

In the fall of 1962, Commack High was brand-new, and the specter of finding my way from class to class would be a major challenge in this sprawling two-story facility with three wings of classrooms, a gym at one far end (in and of itself a new experience—I had never been in a gym class in my life), and shop classrooms and two cafeterias at the other end. That year, CHS housed five grade levels, consisting of 300 to 400 students each.

Beyond the intimidation posed by the enormity of the building, I was entering ninth grade, knowing only my brother Ed, two local guys from the neighborhood, and a cousin who had also moved from Queens the year before. Handicapping me further, or so I thought, was the yet-uncorrected mild-to-moderate hearing loss with which I had been diagnosed about three years earlier, believed, at the time, to have been caused by a severe case of measles at the age of three. The learning and social implications of that condition had been mitigated up to that point by the sheltered school environment in which I managed to function and even excel.

Yet, despite my fears, I managed to develop friends among my classmates. Then, in the spring term, I tried out and was selected for the JV baseball team as a left-handed pitcher with both a wild streak (too many walks) and a nasty curveball. More than anything else, being on a team provided me with an identity that, given the insecurity of a fourteen-year-old, compounded by the anxiety associated with uncorrected hearing loss, was reassuring. In my sophomore year, I pitched JV again. At the end of the season, some of my teammates and I were asked by one of the gym teachers to consider the summer camp position. He didn't have to ask twice. Almost two years after first walking into Commack High School full of trepidations about social isolation and lack of an identity among my peers, I felt gratified. My abnormal urine screening not only introduced the possibility that I had some kind of serious illness, it also meant that I would have to forgo the summer job opportunity that, in my mind, served as confirmation that I was "one of the guys."

Shortly after, I was hospitalized for a week of tests, which included a voiding cystourethrogram in which I lay on an X-ray table fully exposed from the waist down as a doctor and X-ray tech scurried around. One of them produced a catheter that appeared to be the diameter of a garden hose and shoehorned it into my penis. I didn't know whether to be embarrassed or horrified. All I knew was that it hurt like hell. I feared I would never be the same. A bag was attached while Dr. and Mrs. Frankenstein began to introduce what I later knew to be a contrast fluid into my bladder and stopped just before it began to seep from my eye sockets. The urge to pee was excruciating, but I was told, "Now *hold*!" for what seemed to be an eternity while they sadistically took their images. Finally, one of them invited me to pee it out as I lay on the table. If I had had some wits about me, I would have aimed at them.

After a week of that and other lesser tortures, I was discharged. The docs could find nothing structural to account for what was discovered to be both hematuria and proteinuria (red blood cells and protein in my urine). The conclusion was that a bad sore throat the winter before may have been a strep infection that found its way into my kidneys. Fortunately, my kidney's filtering and excretion functions remained normal. In what would now be looked upon as gross malpractice, I was placed on long-term antibiotics, enhanced by a weekly injection of yet another stronger antibiotic. Worse yet, as far as I was concerned, I was not allowed to participate in sports, including gym class in my junior year. The dagger through my heart, though, was that I could not play baseball the following spring.

I was devastated—and pissed (figuratively and literally). Who cared if I had blood cells in my urine? I pitched with my left arm, not my genitourinary system, and I could still snap off a pretty good curveball. On a deeper level, the identity I had secured over two years had been crushed, or so I thought. I still count the first day of baseball the following spring as one of the worst days of my life. At the end of the school day, as my friends on the team headed for tryouts, I headed in the opposite direction to take the school bus home.

Eventually, I developed some side effects from the antibiotics. I learned much later that such long-term antibiotic treatment could have been dangerous and devastating. They were discontinued, and my parents consulted another doctor. In the meantime, Ed, two years my junior, was also discovered to have the same urinary condition. He, too, had hearing loss diagnosed, like mine, at around the age of ten, with similar causation, measles, proposed. We were both hospitalized for three days under the care of a different urologist. I don't recall any torture-like procedures the second time around. The conclusion, though, was that since we each had normal filtering and excretion functions, we should have no physical limitations. There was, at that time, no mention of a relationship between our hearing losses and kidney conditions. I could not then have predicted the course my health would take and the improbable life path on which it would lead.

CHAPTER TWO

## *Making the Team*

In September 1966 I arrived as a freshman at the State University of New York (SUNY) College of Arts and Sciences at Geneseo, a small town nestled on a hillside above the Genesee Valley, thirty miles south of Rochester. I had chosen SUNY Geneseo because it was far away from the hustle and bustle of the New York metro area and had a well-regarded undergraduate major in speech pathology and audiology, a field to which I was attracted because of my own hearing loss. A career working with people who faced the same challenges might prove to be enjoyable and rewarding. I also reasoned that smaller classes would pose fewer difficulties from a hearing standpoint. My hearing had not been corrected by hearing aids at that time, so college academics could prove problematic. But I was resolute in my career choice and felt that the environment at Geneseo would provide me with the best opportunity to pursue it.

I also realized that Geneseo might give me the chance to resume my baseball career, such as it was. The top-level high school ball players tended to gravitate to Southern schools if they intended to play collegiate ball. Geneseo might present an opportunity to resume playing the sport I loved.

I showed up for informal fall baseball practices on Monday, Wednesday, and Friday afternoons. The coach asked each player what our best position might be. I declared myself an outfielder. Not having pitched in over two years, I figured I might have a better chance to make the team as a position player. As a left-handed thrower, I would be restricted to playing either the outfield or first base, but since first basemen are typically tall enough to catch errant throws from other infielders, and I was five-foot-eight on a good day, the outfield was my best hope. I had played outfield in pickup games, so I was confident in my fielding abilities and had decent speed, prerequisites for effective outfield play.

Fall practice went well. I established myself as a legitimate candidate to make the team the following spring. The coach must have observed that I was one of his better defensive outfielders and usually positioned me in centerfield, which had been the position played by the great major leaguers of the era. Growing up in New York City into a family of hereditary Yankee fans who bled white with blue pinstripes, the legacy was clear to me—I would play the position of DiMaggio and Mantle, my father and my baseball idols respectively.

For baseball fans, and Yankee fans in particular, New York was nirvana. In the sixteen seasons between 1949 and 1964, the Yankees won the American league pennant fourteen times. They were part of the story of my childhood and early teen years. One of my earliest memories was watching the last game of the 1953 World Series with my dad on our fifteen-inch black-and-white RCA television as Billy Martin singled to drive home the winning run to beat the Dodgers in the final game. I was five and a half.

In our neighborhood, everyone was either a fan of the Yankees, Brooklyn Dodgers, or New York (baseball) Giants. We developed an affinity for certain players, and for many of us, Mickey Mantle was our guy. In addition to being recognized for his considerable talents on the field, Mick developed a reputation for playing through pain caused by his many injuries. For most of his career, the team trainer would wrap both of his legs before games in ACE bandages, ankles to thighs, so that his knees would not collapse while he was running in the outfield or on the basepaths. His "elbows up" running style suggested that he was often in pain, yet he played through it most of the time and played well.

If Mick ran like that, we would too. Anyone walking past the schoolyard on Thirty-First Street in Astoria during one of our stickball games would have seen a bunch of us running around as if our knees hurt. No one's knees hurt at all. We just wanted to run like Mick. The tenacity with which he played was compelling. I had no way of knowing then that Mick would one day serve as inspiration when I would later be faced with my own health problems.

As baseball workouts ended in late October with a cool fall and early winter descending upon Upstate Western New York, I was determined to make the team the following spring. The one challenge looming large proved not to be on the field, however. I knew that I would have to pass a physical, which would include a urine screening. Nonetheless, I resolved not to let a few milligrams of protein and some rogue red blood cells disrupt my "career" again. I hatched a plan. Just before spring tryouts started, I scheduled my baseball physical at the college infirmary and went into action.

For a full day beforehand, I carried a water bottle everywhere and drank from it constantly. I reasoned that if my urine was primarily water, any protein or red cells would be less likely to show up. I have since been told that urine concentration shouldn't make any difference in terms of detectable hematuria and proteinuria, but for whatever reason, it worked. The doctor gave the litmus stick a quick second look and tossed it in the trash (no medical waste bags in those days). I had passed my physical and could try out for the baseball team. I regret not asking for the litmus stick. It would have made a unique framed memento.

On opening day, I found myself starting in centerfield for my college baseball team, something that looked remote a few short years before. I went on to start in about half of our games. The last two, however, are etched forever in my memory.

A sophomore by the name of Gary D. also tried out for the team that year as a left-handed pitcher. He showed up at tryouts with a new glove, a Rawlings Mickey Mantle model. That glove spoke to me. Back home, on family shopping trips to the Walt Whitman Mall, I would amble over to the E. J. Korvette's sporting goods department and drool over that very same glove on display. It cost $35, an immense sum in the mid-1960s and way beyond my means. When I was in eighth grade, my father had obtained a Spalding Roger Maris fielders glove for me, but it was a kid's toy compared to the Mantle glove, the fingers of which were about two inches longer. The extra length could make a difference in catching or not catching a ball hit to the outfield. It was constructed of high-quality leather that would conform to the wearer's hand and had a deep pocket so a ball landing in it was unlikely to pop out. When Gary D. and his glove failed to make the team, I went out on a financial limb and offered him $25 for it. He declined. I played most of the season with my "kid glove." Then, with two games left and the semester nearing its end, I called him again and asked if he had changed his mind about selling the glove, guessing that he would be short on cash by that time. Never mind that I was about broke too . . . my priorities were in order. He agreed.

I wore it for the first time for our second-to-last game. During pregame outfield practice, I ran in to catch a low, sinking line drive. At the last minute, it sank even lower than I had anticipated. Running at full tilt and with my gloved arm extended out over my right leg to try to make a desperation catch, I anticipated feeling the crack of the ball against my kneecap. I had forgotten that I was wearing my new glove. I looked down. The top of the ball was protruding above the glove's web but secure. My glove had allowed me to make the catch and may have protected me from injury had I missed.

Our team won that game. I had two hits and played well in the outfield. My glove and I were in center field to start the last game of the season.

We were a mediocre team with a losing record. Our opponent that day was SUNY Oswego, the first-place team in the SUNY Athletic Conference. A win didn't seem to be in the cards. Yet, spring had at long last arrived in western New York, and it was a beautiful afternoon for a ball game. More to enjoy a warm sunny day than to see us play, a large crowd assembled to take the game in. I responded by striking out my first three times at bat against a tough right-handed curveballer. Despite that, it turned out to be the most memorable game of my college baseball career, which tells you all you need to know about my college baseball career.

We had our best pitcher on the mound that day, a lanky right-hander who threw high eighties with a decent curve and changeup. Against all odds, we held a 4-3 lead in the seventh inning. Oswego had a runner on first with one out and a right-handed hitter at bat. I positioned myself a few steps into left-center, anticipating that he was likely to pull the ball toward that side of the field. He got hold of a pitch and drove it deep in the air to the left. Mike G., our left fielder, was a good hitter but a mediocre defensive outfielder. I knew that Mike wasn't going to catch it. If the ball got by Mike and me, it would allow the runner on first to score and place the hitter on second or third in scoring position. The game was at stake.

I put my head down and ran full speed to the spot where I instinctively thought the ball might land. I looked up and saw Mike flailing around, in no position to make the catch as the ball sped on its downward arc. Sometimes outfielders seem able to will the ball to stay in the air until they can catch it. There is no other way to explain the fact that the ball seemed to hang for a split second longer than it would have. At the last minute, I dove with my gloved hand and arm outstretched. The ball plopped into my glove and stayed there as I skidded, head, chest, and arms first, along the outfield grass.

We escaped the inning with no runs scored against us. I batted one more time and managed to work a walk against my pitching nemesis. We went on to win the game 4-3, beating the first-place team and giving our fans a good game.

I still have my glove. About fifteen years ago, JoAnne had the rawhide stitching reworked. It sits on one of our bookshelves next to a biography of Mickey Mantle. A ball is tucked neatly in the pocket, just in case a game should break out in front of me, "the hope that springs eternal in the human breast." [1]

---

1  "Casey at the Bat", Ernest Thayer, 1888.

My Rawlings Mickey Mantle glove

My team, spring 1962, Astoria, Queens, New York. My dad, upper left, was our coach. I'm next to him.

CHAPTER THREE

*Out the Window*

Early in my sophomore year at SUNY Geneseo, I met JoAnne Havens, now JoAnne Gance for the past fifty-five years and the love of my life, the one person who has been by my side "in sickness and in health" through all of this. We married three weeks after graduation in 1970 and, two months later, moved from Upstate New York to Kalamazoo, Michigan, where I had secured a graduate fellowship in the master's program in speech pathology and audiology at Western Michigan University. Our son, Dave, was born in February 1973, and by the end of 1974, we awaited the birth of our second child due in June the following year.

We eventually settled in southeastern Pennsylvania, where I served as audiologist and speech pathologist of the newly established Speech and Hearing Center at Reading Hospital. At some point, I decided that, as a young father with parental and family responsibilities, it would be a good idea to get a physical exam and establish myself with a primary care doctor. In the back of my mind was the possibility that the proteinuria/hematuria issue would raise its head, but by this time, there was no baseball physical to worry about, so I let the chips fall where they may or—more precisely—let the pee flow how it may without the benefit of carrying a water bottle around for days. The doctor I saw was Reading Hospital's chief resident in family practice, an astute clinician who zeroed in on my urinalysis results and hearing loss. It was the first time anyone had put the two together, although in my studies of syndromic[2] hearing loss at WMU, I had discovered an entity called Alport syndrome. At the time, though, I was still adhering to the narrative that my hearing loss had been caused by measles and my abnormal urine findings by a strep infection that had altered my kidneys enough to produce abnormal urinalysis results. The doctor seemed suspicious of that scenario and referred me for a kidney biopsy to settle the matter. I agreed.

In January 1975 I was admitted to the Reading Hospital for the procedure, which involved insertion of a biopsy needle into my right kidney as I lay belly down on an examining table. It was not terribly painful, although there was no anesthesia that I recall.

I still have a copy of the pathology report. It showed a "mild and focal degree of mesangial proliferation consistent with hereditary nephritis." In other words, the strep infection theory was out the window. I had a type of microstructural pathology in my kidneys that was consistent with an inherited kidney problem rather than from damage that might have come from a strep infection. This, in turn, raised several questions. From whom had I inherited this condition, and, more importantly, what were the chances that either of our kids would inherit it? There was also the issue of my long-term prognosis.

As far as the former was concerned, there was no history of early-onset kidney failure on either side of my family, although there was a fuzzy history of my maternal grandfather having a kidney removed in midlife for unknown reasons. He also had obvious uncorrected hearing loss as far back as I could remember. However, he lived to be eighty-one and died of abdominal cancer. My mother also had hearing loss, diagnosed in her early thirties, but no symptoms of kidney disease at the time. The salient conclusion was that, inasmuch as there was no family history of early-onset kidney failure, the long-term prognosis was unlikely to be an issue either for me or my brother Ed, a conclusion that turned out to be

---

2   Groups of symptoms that occur together due to genetic anomalies.

mistaken. The hearing loss aspect of Alport was, by now, managed with hearing aids. However, I would need to have annual checkups, which would include lab work to monitor my kidney function.[3]

---

3    Years later in my position as audiologist at Berks ENT Surgical Associates, I saw a male patient in his late forties whose kidneys failed about a decade earlier. He also had hearing loss that had an audiometric configuration similar to mine. He had been told that he likely had a strep infection at one time that settled in his kidneys. Yet, like me, he never had a throat culture for confirmation of that diagnosis. His correct diagnosis was almost certainly sensorineural hearing loss and end-stage renal failure secondary to Alport syndrome. It illustrates the degree to which medical ignorance about unusual syndromic conditions still exists.

## CHAPTER FOUR

## *A Kick in the Gut*

When I was thirty years old, my passion for baseball gave way to what would become a commitment to fitness, the core element of which was running. That evolution was prompted in part by an amusing episode that occurred in the summer of 1978 while visiting JoAnne's family in Elmira, New York. At the time, though, it didn't feel very amusing.

Like most families who live a distance apart, our get-togethers featured extended dinners in which the repartee was enjoyed as much as the food and drink. One evening, after spending a warm, humid day on the golf course with Jo's dad and dinner with her parents, sister, brother, and their spouses, I developed a painful cramp in my right hamstring that caught me by surprise. I stood up suddenly to attempt to stretch it out when my right quadricep (the predominant muscle in the front of the upper leg) also kicked up in a cramp. I tried to sit back down again, pushing my chair away from the table and attempting the physically impossible task of stretching antagonistic muscles, to which effort a muscle in my left leg immediately went into a painful spasm. Those at the table reacted with concern for about two seconds, then with great mirth as I writhed in pain, the cramps proving utterly intractable for what, at the time, seemed like an eternity but was only a matter of twenty or thirty seconds. Finally, one of the three nurses in the family was able to drum up some compassion between guffaws and offer me some salt right from the shaker. The cramps began to subside as my pain level was reduced from excruciating to tolerable. I didn't mind the fun at my expense and had to admit I must have been quite a sight. No doubt it would have made an appearance on social media if it happened now.

The episode, though, proved to be instructive. Even at the tender age of thirty, I was prompted to assess my fitness level and reasoned that, as my baseball/softball days ebbed, I would have to replace that physical activity with something else.

The late 1970s and early '80s saw the emergence of the running boom. With it, races ranging in length from 5 kilometers (3.1 miles) to the marathon (26.2 miles) and even longer began popping up in many localities across the country. Within a few weeks of my cramping episode, I started doing some short jogs around the neighborhood and on the local high school track. Sometime later, a doctor I knew gave me an entry form for the first annual Reading Hospital Road Run, a 10K (6.2 miles) event to be held in May of 1979. The late Dr. George Sheehan, a cardiologist and acknowledged philosophical guru of the running movement, had written that the difference between jogging and running was a race entry form, a matter of attitude rather than speed. I signed up.

Thus began my participation in road races of all distances up to and including the marathon, a pastime enhanced when we moved from West Lawn, PA, to Wernersville, PA, five miles down the road. There I became close friends with other runners who lived in the area, in particular Scott Giacobbe and George Michael (I would later dub our running triumvirate "The Wernersville Track Club"). Our wives also ran to one extent or another, and our kids often participated in the "fun runs" associated with some of the races.

I ran my first full marathon in Philadelphia on a rainy late fall day in 1982, accompanied and cheered on by JoAnne, our kids Dave and Amy, and Rita. Among some in the running community, there was the opinion that running a marathon served as an indication of supreme health. I was soon to find out otherwise.

In late February 1983, a friend who was the administrative director of Reading Hospital's lab services asked me if I would allow one of their phlebotomists to take a blood sample. The lab had just received a new piece of equipment that would facilitate an increased number of blood tests from a single vial. He wanted to compare the results of presumed "normals" to those norms proposed by the manufacturer's specifications. A few days later he called me. My cholesterol was 343! At the time, the top normal blood cholesterol was 250. So much for my presumption of supreme health.

I hadn't had a physical exam in almost three years. I was a distance runner who had just run my first marathon. Why would I need to see a doctor for anything? That cholesterol number rattled my complacency. I made an appointment with my physician.

Thus, it served as a kick-in-the-gut to find out that my kidney condition had begun to deteriorate irreversibly. I found out that I was spilling high amounts of protein in my urine, and my liver was responding by generating some proteins of its own to compensate. The altered liver metabolism was also dumping elevated levels of cholesterol into my blood. But the key finding was that my kidneys had started to fail, and I was told that I would be in "end-stage renal failure" within two to five years, at which time I would have to start dialysis or have a transplant.

I left the doctor's office in a fog. When I returned to my office, I called JoAnne to relay the news. It hit her as hard as it had hit me. There was no point in carrying on a lengthy phone conversation about the considerable implications. We would discuss it later that evening at home, after the kids were in bed. She suggested that I should get a second opinion. However, I had no illusions that the lab results could have been a mistake. I was part of the medical establishment, and, while I knew that doctors were wrong occasionally, knowledge of my underlying condition and the degree to which my blood and urine tests lined up and reinforced each other left no room for doubt.

To say that JoAnne and I were shaken to the core was an understatement. Our daughter, Amy, who was born in 1975, was not yet eight, and our son, Dave, had just turned ten. Our family's future was suddenly turned upside down. JoAnne and I decided not to share this news with our kids. There were just too many unknowns with which we felt they should not be burdened. That night we laid in each other's arms and cried ourselves to sleep . . . if we slept at all. On other nights, each of us shed tears silently on our own. It was a scary time.

We told a few friends. Scott and George were my two closest running friends. If I could talk about my diagnosis while clicking off seven-and-a-half-minute miles, how sick could I be?

My doctor had mentioned dialysis or a transplant as management options when my kidneys eventually reached the point at which I would be unable to function on a day-to-day basis. He painted a relatively positive picture, pointing out that many people lived close-to-normal lives with either option. He stressed, however, that prudent medical management, including blood pressure control, would be critical to long-term health and survival.

Coincidentally, the obstetrician who delivered Amy had been a dialysis patient for years and continued an active medical practice. My doctor suggested that we contact him to learn more about dialysis as a lifestyle option. JoAnne called his office, and he agreed to meet with us after hours. It would be our first true interaction with a person on dialysis who was dealing with the same health challenges that would eventually confront me. We found the discussion helpful, yet the stark reality that our lifestyles would one day be substantially altered still seemed not to have totally sunk in.

It definitely sank in about a month later when we traveled to Long Island for a cousin's wedding. As I watched her being escorted down the aisle by her father, I was gripped by the distinct possibility that I might not be around when it was Amy's turn. The numbers were sobering. They showed that, out of a population of one hundred maintenance dialysis patients, five would be expected to die every year. Amy was then not quite eight years old. If I chose dialysis, I had less than a fifty-fifty chance of survival until she was likely to get married. There was a significant possibility that I might not be a very vibrant presence as my children grew into adulthood. I might not even live that long. There were so many unknowns.

In June of that year, we drove down to Boynton Beach, Florida, to visit my parents. It would be our first visit with them since we were told that my kidneys would fail. After a full day on the road, we stopped at a nondescript exit in South Carolina and checked into a motel to use the pool, have dinner, and get a good night's sleep before completing our journey the next day. While JoAnne, Dave, and Amy headed outside for a swim, I stayed in the room for a few moments to gather my thoughts. A Gideon Bible sat on a table at bedside. I opened to a page at random. Psalm 139:12 looked back at me: *"even the darkness will not be dark to you; the night will shine like the day . . ."*

I don't know if there is a conventional interpretation of that passage, but at that moment, I understood it to mean that, somehow, I would overcome this adversity and running would be a part of it. Then I changed into my bathing suit and went outside to join JoAnne and the kids.

My brother Ed had flown to Florida from California, where he had relocated in the mid-seventies. I would take this opportunity to tell him about my medical news so he would be forewarned. If this was going to happen to me, it was going to happen to him too. One day at the beach, I took him aside.

"Ed," I began, "that old story that our hearing losses were caused by measles and our kidney abnormalities by strep infections, it was bull. We have a hereditary condition called Alport syndrome. My kidneys have begun to fail, and yours will too."

I stressed that, based on my doctor's recommendations, he should be followed medically to check his condition, otherwise his blood pressure could get out of control and eventually result in cardiovascular consequences. He nodded but said nothing more.

We continued to keep the news from my parents. We would tell them when the time came, whenever that might be.

## CHAPTER FIVE

## *The New York City Marathon*

I vowed to keep running. Thus, it was at lunchtime, two hours after being confronted with a bleak medical diagnosis and still reeling emotionally, that I decided "screw it" and went out for a run. It would turn out to be predictive of my approach to dealing with this challenge for years to come. A few years earlier, I had adopted the habit of running at lunch. From noon to one o'clock every weekday, a handful of pseudo-jocks descended on a cramped locker room in the bowels of Reading Hospital's maintenance wing, where we changed into athletic gear and spent the better part of our lunch hour indulging our athletic fantasies. The tennis players among us engaged in spirited matches on the hospital's nearby courts, while others went out for a three-to-five-mile run. I joined the latter crew.

About a week after receiving my diagnosis, I joined Scott, George, and a few other running buddies in the St. Patty's ten-miler, the runner's Rite of Impending Spring in Berks and surrounding counties. I would not be defeated if I could put one foot in front of the other. In retrospect, "running through it" may have served as my own personal vehicle for denial, but at least it was a healthy denial. Among those of us who were in the throes of running hedonism, there was an adage that you could "run through" certain injuries or conditions. I vowed to run through renal failure for as long as I could.

Seven months later, on October 23, 1983, I found myself lining up with 16,000 other runners at the Staten Island side of the Verrazano Bridge for the start of the New York City Marathon. I owed my presence there that day, ironically enough, to Alport syndrome.

Running New York had been my ultimate running goal for several years. Having grown up in Queens, returning to the city of my birth as a participant in one of the world's premier sporting events held great appeal for me. It was there that my love of sports was established. From my youth, athletics had played a role in my life. My diagnosis the previous March added some urgency to my quest. If I was going to run the New York Marathon, I'd better do it while I was still able.

However, gaining entry was practically impossible. The race had grown in popularity and was in full swing by the early eighties. This was due in part to national TV coverage that capitalized on the sheer spectacle of thousands of runners traversing the five boroughs of the greatest city in the world. That year, the sponsoring organization, the New York Road Runners Club, had planned to accept 16,000 entrants. There would be over 80,000 applicants.

The first 8,000 completed applications received would be accepted; the remaining 72,000 would be thrown into a lottery. All applicants were required to send a self-addressed, stamped envelope to the New York Road Runners Club, postmarked no earlier than midnight, June 1. The club would then send out the entry forms and accept the first 8,000 that were returned.

This system favored New York City residents, thousands of whom queued up outside Grand Central Post Office on the evening of May 31 and deposited their stamped, self-addressed envelopes at the stroke of midnight. To get into the race, I concocted a scheme. I managed to get my envelope postmarked "June 1" by a sympathetic postage meter but mailed it May 31. When I received the application back, I mailed it "next-day air special handling." Despite my efforts, I was not one of the first 8,000. I learned a month later that I wasn't one of the second 8,000 either. It was time for plan B.

I wrote a letter to Fred Lebow, the president of the New York Road Runners Club, explaining that, as a New York City native, it was my dream to run the New York Marathon. However, I went on, I had a progressive kidney condition. If I couldn't run New York this year, I might never run it. My doctor wrote an accompanying letter confirming my story. July turned into August. I heard nothing. Then, one day in late August, I received a letter from the race appeals committee, extending an invitation to run the New York Marathon. My dream would become a reality. I rushed over to Scott's house to share the good news. His immediate reaction was to proclaim that the Giacobbe family would join our family on our epic trip to New York. Scott had battled a few of his own seemingly chronic running injuries that year and wasn't able to train for this kind of event. Even though the two of us had talked about running New York together some day, he was as excited about being a part of my support crew/cheering section as I was about being in the race.

On the morning of Saturday, October 22, Rita, who had taken a position as radiology technologist at Reading Hospital about seven years earlier, joined the Gance and Giacobbe families as we drove to the Big Apple. After checking into our adjoining rooms at the City Squire Hotel, we set out to tour Manhattan, including a subway ride to Thirty-Fourth Street to see the Empire State Building. From the observation deck on the eighty-second floor, it was possible to look out over the city and see the entire marathon course. As a kid, I would occasionally look over at that iconic structure from our apartment building in Astoria, never remotely imagining that someday I would be looking down from it at the scene of one of the world's greatest sporting events and that I would be a participant.

The prescribed formula for running a marathon stipulates that the runner spend the day before the race in sedentary mode. For me, the day before the New York Marathon was anything but sedentary as we obtained my runners packet at the race expo and checked out some of the sights and sounds of Midtown Manhattan. I hadn't entered the race to run a fast time and knew that, in the latter half of the race, I would pay for Saturday's excursions. However, I was the only one of our group who knew my way around the city. We walked many miles that day, completely counter to the conventional wisdom of sitting with feet elevated. In another blatant violation of tried-and-true pre-marathon preparations, we forsook the usual pasta dinner and, instead, stopped at a New York deli for a hot pastrami sandwich on rye with a kosher dill.

That night, I didn't sleep a wink. Scott had insisted that I drink plenty of Perrier to load up on minerals my body would need the next day. I consumed three sixteen-ounce bottles and consequently spent most of the night burping and peeing, sometimes simultaneously. I didn't exactly feel fresh in the morning. Yet, adrenalin went a long way toward relegating fatigue to the back of my mind.

Unlike Saturday, which had been a warm fall day, Sunday dawned raw, damp, and overcast, with a one-hundred-percent chance of rain. JoAnne and I rose early, around 5 a.m. I was to catch a runner's bus at Lincoln Center by 7 a.m. for the ride to the starting area on Staten Island. We had anticipated a crowded hotel restaurant that morning, so, in her usual pragmatic efficiency, JoAnne had brought along an electric coffee maker and coffee cake. We would have a light breakfast in our room before going over to Lincoln Center, leaving Rita and the kids to sleep.

Just as JoAnne poured the coffee, there was a faint tapping at the door between our rooms. JoAnne heard, "Bobby, Bobby . . . are you ready?" I went over and opened the door. Scott burst in, put his arms around me, and said, "Bobby, Bobby, this is it . . . this is your big day! Are you ready? Did you sleep? How do you feel? Are you nervous?" all in a whisper of sorts so as not to wake up the kids.

"Scott, I'm fine. Sit down, relax, and have some coffee cake and coffee."

"Oh, I can't," he replied, clutching his abdomen, "I never eat before a race." He continued to pace the room like a caged tiger.

"Scott." We laughed. "You're not the one running." But it made no difference. He still wouldn't eat anything. As we recounted the incident later, his wife, Judy said that when she was in labor with each of their children, Scott would have labor pains. I suppose whether you are running a marathon or having a baby, it's great to have that kind of empathetic support.

It was still dark as JoAnne and Scott accompanied me to catch my bus at Lincoln Center. As I lined up to board, I effectively lost contact with my support crew, much like lunar astronauts lost contact with mission control as they circled the far side of the moon. I realized that running a marathon was not a solo endeavor. The encouragement and motivation supplied by friends and family were as much a part of the effort as were the fifty-mile weeks. I could no more have attempted a marathon without their support than I could attempt it without running shoes. Although I was one of a cast of 16,000 taking part in this extravaganza, as the bus pulled away into the gloomy Manhattan canyons, I felt very much alone.

By then, darkness had given way to a tepid, all-pervasive gray that engulfed the city. I peered out the bus windows and began to wonder whether I belonged here. I had completed my first marathon a year earlier as a reasonably fit runner; running a marathon had been the appropriate culmination of my running efforts up to then. Now my motivation was different. In the emotional isolation of the bus ride to Staten Island, I began to see that the challenge of the marathon had become, for me, a vehicle with which I could respond to the specter of a chronic, progressive illness. Perhaps I was still not accepting the fact that the course of my condition was entirely beyond my control, and I had focused on the challenge of the New York Marathon as a substitute for the foreboding challenge of my illness. *Is this*, I wondered, *a valid reason for running a marathon? If not, will I be able to meet the physical demands imposed by running 26.2 miles?* I discreetly looked around at other runners. I saw that, while some appeared at least as trim and fit as I was, others certainly didn't. As the bus rolled through the dim streets, I slowly gained assurance that there were 16,000 motivations for running the New York Marathon that day. Mine was no less valid than most, perhaps more valid than many.

After a forty-five-minute bus ride, we arrived at Fort Wadsworth, an active army installation that served as a staging area on the Staten Island side of the Verrazzano-Narrows Bridge. Fort Wadsworth was located adjacent to the wide toll plaza where the race would start. About a dozen circus-size tents had been erected; one would be my home for the next three hours. There were also refreshment tents where runners could get a hot cup of coffee, numerous porta potties, and, consistent with New York's penchant for having the biggest and best of everything, a 200-foot-long trough dubbed "the world's longest urinal." What more could a runner ask for?

I found my way into a tent already occupied by several hundred runners, most of whom were reclining on the damp ground, their heads resting on duffel bags that served as pillows. Some slept or appeared to be sleeping; others read or appeared to be reading. Copies of the *Wall Street Journal* and *Businessweek* strewn about suggested that New York Marathoners were largely a white-collar crowd. I eventually staked out my spot by stretching out to rest and hopefully make up for some of the sleep I didn't get the night before. Who was I kidding? I was too keyed up to sleep. I had also brought along a paperback book but found myself staring at the same page for minutes at a time. I finally resorted to taking occasional walks, did some stretching, had one or two cups of coffee, and visited the world's longest urinal. How ironic . . . someone whose kidneys were beginning to fail using the largest urinal in the world! As I stood making my contribution to the impressive yellow current, I postulated whether anyone else similarly engaged had a progressive kidney ailment like mine, but once I pulled up my sweatpants, I found my mind occupied with the challenge of running 26.2 miles through the streets of New York.

About a half hour before race time, an invisible Fort Wadsworth Big Brother blared an announcement that runners could deposit their duffle bags back into the bus that had brought them. They could then be claimed in Central Park after the race. I tossed mine in and, along with 16,000 others, made my way over to the gates leading to the toll plaza. As the throng began to funnel through, I checked my runner's watch. It was 10:30.

For three hours, most of us had been trying to relax and hold our emotions in check to save all possible energy for the task at hand. Now, as helicopters circled noisily overhead, the adrenaline surge was almost dizzying. In past years, I had watched this impressive spectacle unfold on TV. Now, thanks to Alport syndrome, I was a part of it. I thought about JoAnne, Rita, Scott, Judy, and the kids. They had enthusiastically accompanied me on my adventure. My parents would be watching the telecast on TV from their home in Florida, which, just then, didn't seem like a bad place to be. Growing up in New York, my dad had been very active in sports, as was his dad, my uncles, and my cousins. In addition, Rita had garnered a room full of trophies in her high school athletic career. Now, here I was . . . carrying on the family tradition on one of the biggest sports stages in the world.

With less than a minute to go before the start, I set the chronometer on my runner's watch to 00'00". The other runners did the same, as though on command from the running gods, even though we all knew that digital clocks would be displaying elapsed time every mile. Runners are, above all, creatures of habit.

To start most races, the starter fires a starter's pistol. In New York, they fire a cannon. I looked up at the bridge's towers; they were surrounded by fog and mist. A light rain was falling. Despite the gloomy weather, the mood was upbeat, and there was much chatter among the runners as we began our long journey. The Verrazzano-Narrows Bridge was, at that time, the longest suspension bridge in the world. I had read that such bridges must be constructed so that they give somewhat with wind and other forces, such as 32,000 stampeding feet on the upper level and a full complement of car and truck traffic on the lower.

I can report that the Verrazzano Bridge does, in fact, move! The first expansion joint is about halfway between the base and the first tower. As I approached it, I had the distinct impression that, for several strides, the pavement wasn't exactly where I thought it should have been when my foot struck it. I must not have been the only one who thought so because a whole pocket of runners around me shouted "whoa" simultaneously as though we were riding a two-mile-long steel and concrete bucking bronco suspended 250 feet above lower New York Bay. Not surprisingly, the pace picked up for a few seconds. Some minutes later, I approached the one-mile digital clock at midspan. It read 11:35. The lead runners had covered the same distance in five minutes. The second mile took us down into Brooklyn. It was comforting to reach level ground again.

Despite the rain, which had increased in intensity since the start, most of the course in that borough of neighborhoods was lined with huge crowds, and the scenery took on the expected ethnic flavor, highlighted by black-garbed Hasidic Jews at the eight-mile point in the Williamsburg neighborhood. A stereotype paints them as reserved, even somber, but they were quite vocal and enthusiastic in support of the runners. I noticed that there were no women among them. Perhaps Orthodox rules forbade them from participating in such an activity. Then again, maybe the women had the good sense to stay out of the rain!

The halfway point came in the center of the Pulaski Bridge, which spans hopelessly polluted Newtown Creek and separates Brooklyn and Queens. If reincarnation applies to bodies of water, Newtown Creek deserves a better fate in the next life. Somewhere over its murky waters, the first twinge of a leg cramp appeared. I fought it off but knew that cramping this early in a marathon didn't bode well. It had taken me about one hour and fifty minutes to run the first half of the race. There was no doubt in my mind that the second half would take longer.

In contrast to the cheering crowds of Brooklyn, the streets in the two-mile stretch of an industrial section of Queens were starkly deserted. I was glad to begin making my way up the approach ramp to the Queensborough Bridge, also known as the Fifty-Ninth Street Bridge, made famous by the Simon and Garfunkel song. It would take the runners over the East River. As we ascended, the view of the Midtown Manhattan skyline was spectacular even on this dismal day. The UN sat next to the river with the Chrysler and Empire State Buildings joining other skyscrapers to form an impressive backdrop. From the river below, fireboats greeted the runners by spraying huge arcs of red, white, and blue water high into the air. For a moment, I forgot about my aching legs.

Not long after reaching the span's midpoint, we began our descent into the heart of the city. I became vaguely aware of a noise that I couldn't identify. It seemed to start as a low rumble that increased in intensity with each stride. The course made a series of three quick 90-degree left turns that brought us back under the ramp, over which we had just traversed, and onto First Avenue heading north. Once we emerged, the source of the noise became obvious. First Avenue was lined with spectators, eight- to ten-deep, all of them screaming at the top of their lungs. The din was deafening, even to a person already half deaf! Some had brought orange slices to pass out to the runners. I gladly grabbed a few, hoping they would help forestall my leg cramps. Lined with luxury apartments, restaurants, and shops, First Avenue reflected upscale New York. Each year since the Marathon adopted its five-borough format in 1976, it had been the gathering point of tens of thousands of New Yorkers who formed the city's unofficial welcoming committee. It also marked mile point sixteen. There were a little over ten to go.

As I plodded on through the rain and headed north toward East Harlem and the Bronx, the cheers of the First Avenue crowd gradually faded. By mile eighteen, boarded-up storefronts had given the course a different face. The brief adrenalin kick provided by the crowd had gradually disappeared, and, as the twenty-mile point approached, the marathon had once again become a bleak affair. Both my mind and body screamed for relief as the course crossed the Willits Avenue Bridge, which took us over the Harlem River, from Manhattan into the Bronx. The leg cramps I had managed to fight off from miles thirteen to eighteen had become intractable. I had been taking fluids on the run at almost all the previous water stations, but this time I came to a stop to take a cup of water from a race volunteer. The cramps persisted. I resumed running, now down to about a ten-minute-per-mile pace.

We crossed back into Manhattan and headed south toward Central Park. Few spectators were taking in the action, although a young African American boy, whom I judged to be about ten, ran over to me and gave me a high-five. I don't know how I managed to raise my arm up to meet his, but I appreciated his effort as much as he appreciated mine. Early in the race, I tried to avoid puddles to keep my shoes and socks dry, but by now, they were hopelessly soggy, so I sloshed through the puddles like everyone else, knowing that the energy expenditure required to avoid them was prohibitive.

Eventually, we made a right into Central Park at mile twenty-three, continuing to head south on a winding park road punctuated by huge hills. At least they seemed huge after running twenty-three miles. In reality, the elevation gain on the largest of them was probably no more than eight feet. With the column of runners now compressed from the width of a wide city street to that of a narrow park road, and the crowd growing in size and loudness with every turn, the marathon once again began to assume the identity of a race instead of a survival march. I tried to respond to this new source of inspiration by increasing my speed like other runners around me, but my legs wouldn't cooperate. How frustrating! The overwhelming sense of fatigue had subsided as the excitement of the last few miles increased, yet my cramped legs wouldn't allow me to take advantage of my newfound energy.

At twenty-five miles, we exited the park at its southeast corner and headed west toward Columbus Circle. Once again, cheering crowds lined the course. I knew from my watch that I would be very close to a four-hour time, and while I had no particular target in mind, I very much wanted to run the marathon in less than that. With a half-mile to go, we made a right turn at the circle and headed back into the park for the final uphill segment. By now, large crowds lined both sides of the course, screaming hysterically. Bleachers were packed with supporters along the final quarter mile, and I could see the finish line banner up ahead. I tried to throw in one final surge, but my cramped legs wouldn't let me. With the cheers of thousands ringing in my ears, I crossed the finish line four hours and forty seconds after beginning my wet 26.2-mile odyssey through the streets of New York. For me, the New York City Marathon was finally, mercifully, over.

I was grateful to be able to stop running, but even walking through the chutes was painful. A few yards after I crossed the finish line, a volunteer wrapped a mylar sheet around me, encouraging me to keep moving. Several yards later, I was handed a box lunch, while another volunteer hung a pewter medal around my neck, all the time gently prodding, "Keep moving."

The din of the finish line gradually faded and was replaced by an eerie silence, rhythmically punctuated by the swish-swish of the mylar wraps. I looked around and saw that I was one of a line of bent, exhausted figures slowly making our way to wherever some unseen master was herding us. No one talked. It was, by now, almost three o'clock, and the rain continued unabated. The scene was becoming Kafkaesque. After a half mile, we approached a clearing in which large letters had been placed atop lampposts. The idea, evidently, was to find the post with the first letter of your last name, if you could even remember it at this point. Your family would meet you there.

I found a G pole and stood around it for a few minutes, which, at the time, seemed like hours. The mylar sheet helped a little, but my body had little fuel left for warmth. A sense of desperation began to creep in as I wondered if my crew would find me. Would I have to wander for hours looking for them? Here I was, standing somewhere in Central Park, New York, on a cold, wet afternoon, wearing running shorts and having run 26.2 miles through the rain. What a stupid idea! I must be nuts. And not only had I spent four hours at this soggy enterprise, I had also dragged my family and another family with me. I thought for sure they must all be cursing me soundly by now. Hopefully, they had watched most of the race in their warm, dry hotel room.

After what seemed like an eternity, they found me. Led by JoAnne, all eight hugged me simultaneously, ignoring the fact that I was soaking wet. They seemed deliriously excited to have been part of this amazing, wondrous adventure. Jo miraculously produced a set of dry clothes. She ordered Judy, Amy, Kristen, and Rita not to peek as she, Dave, Danny, and Scott stripped every stitch of wet clothes off me and got me into something warm and dry. When I finally stopped shivering, I could see by their faces that they had had a great day.

We began to make our way through the park. Everyone wanted to know about my race. I was able to recount bits and pieces, but my mind was still too numb to recall details. My crew, however, filled me in on their day.

It seemed like a lifetime ago when JoAnne and Scott saw me off at Lincoln Center. From there, instead of returning to the hotel, they walked over to the finish line area to scout around and saw that the bleachers that had been temporarily erected along the last few hundred yards of the course were rapidly filling up. They hurried back to the hotel, roused the others, rushed over to the finish line area, and grabbed front-row seats. Best of all, they found themselves next to a person who had brought along a portable TV, and they were able to watch the whole race. And while the rain had followed the runners all the way from Staten Island, it had only begun to rain at the finish line about an hour before I crossed it.

We took the subway back to the hotel, grabbed something to eat, headed for the parking garage, and waited for the attendant to bring our cars. I was beginning to appreciate that this had been a very special day for all of us. Judy and Scott loved it, and it meant a great deal to me that they cared enough to share my experience. JoAnne was absolutely beaming with pride. I knew that I was fortunate to have a wife who supported me to the hilt in this insane adventure. Even the kids had a great time on their first visit to New York. And Rita. Rita was my link to the family athletic tradition of celebrating life by lacing on a pair of athletic shoes. It had been an unforgettable day for all of us.

Our cars arrived. As we were about to pile in, Scott and I shook hands. For me, it was a special moment. Deep down, only another runner could appreciate what this day meant. We had run many miles together, mostly in the comradeship of training, some in the competition of a race. Then he said something I've never forgotten.

"This was your dream, Bobby. Some people never accomplish their dream." We began the long drive home.

Over the next few weeks, I found myself in an emotional funk. I no longer had the New York Marathon to look forward to. It had been my focus for months and part of my running plans for years. Now it was over. It would be years before I would truly understand the emotions of those days.

By entering and training for the New York Marathon, I was providing myself with a vehicle for denial. The marathon was something I could attack and conquer. However, I had no control of the genetic condition that would cause my kidneys to fail in the not-too-distant future. With the race behind me, the sobering reality of my condition began to set in. I had run 26.2 miles. I had returned to the city of my birth to complete the world's greatest footrace. In Scott's words, I had accomplished my dream. But somewhere in the essence of my being lurked the grim reality that the real race had just begun.

"The New York Marathon had been my ultimate running goal for years."

George Michael, me, Scott Giacobbe, "The Wernersville Track Club," 1984

## CHAPTER SIX

## *Hard Pills to Swallow*

The evening of Memorial Day less than a year later, I received a phone call from my mother. My father had passed away suddenly at a party in their condo complex in Boynton Beach, Florida. He was sixty-one. I knew that he had battled high cholesterol for years and had a history of recurrent chest pain from the time he was in his early forties. I had always regarded myself as a clone of my dad. I was an inch or two taller and had a slightly slimmer build. What settled in my mind, however, was that I, like him, had a cholesterol problem.

My dad's father died of congestive heart failure twenty-four years earlier at the age of sixty-six. Clearly, I was not going to inherit any genes for longevity from my paternal male ancestors. About eight months later, my mother's youngest brother died of heart disease in his mid-fifties. Then her sixty-five-year-old brother died less than a year later during heart surgery. In addition to having inherited a progressive kidney ailment from my mother's side of the family, it was now beginning to look as though early demise from heart disease could be targeting me from both sides. I began to feel as though the genetic powers-that-be had drawn a target on my chest, and, sooner or later, I would be next.

I vowed to keep running. Combined with diet management and blood pressure monitoring, running was the one way I might gain some control over the course of my condition and give myself the satisfaction that I was fighting off challenges to my health and longevity as aggressively as I could.

In early April 1985 I signed up for a 10K road race aptly named "The Low Gear Run." The previous December, I had run my PR (personal record) 10K. The Low Gear Run wasn't going to witness another PR by me or anyone else. A mile and a half into the race, the course featured an 800-foot elevation gain, a similar drop over the next mile and a half, another nasty climb of about the same magnitude, and a gradual downhill finish. With about a half mile to go, I saw that a runner who had been ahead of me had collapsed on the course. A cluster of people around him were working feverishly on his limp body. By the time I crossed the finish line, an ambulance had been summoned, and word spread that things didn't look good. Later, we found out that he was pronounced dead shortly after he reached the hospital.

When I arrived at work at Reading Hospital the following Monday, I sought out further information about him. In those days prior to the passage of health information privacy regulations (HIPAA), I was able to ascertain that he was thirty years old and had been diagnosed with familial hyperlipidemia, meaning that his genetic makeup resulted in extremely high levels of cholesterol and other blood fats. This was before medications were available to treat such conditions. To me, the implications were clear: A young male runner with high cholesterol died way too soon from heart disease. I couldn't help but wonder when my turn would come.

At the same time, my blood pressure was beginning to creep up, although not to the point at which my physician felt treatment was necessary. However, with my slim build and a runner's strong pulse, I was often able to sense my heartbeat and found that unnerving.

A few weeks later I was giving a lecture to a group of students in Reading Hospital's School of Nursing. Part of the way through, I began to feel my pulse with an intensity that made it seem as though my heart would explode out of my chest, provoking anxiety that, in turn, made my sense of my own pulse even stronger. I managed to finish my lecture, rushed back to my office to tell our secretary to cancel my appointments for the rest of the day, and hurriedly made my way over to the emergency room. After a series of tests, including an EKG, I was told that I was experiencing a panic attack and sent home on a tranquilizer. It was clear that I was carrying a lot of anxiety and needed to start dealing with it.

I was put in touch with a counselor at Reading Hospital's Mental Health Treatment Center who, as it happened, was a little younger than me and had been on dialysis due to end-stage kidney failure secondary to an inflammatory condition that was then referred to as "Bright's Disease." He was awaiting a kidney transplant in a few months. As our session began, he simply asked what brought me to see him. As I started to tell my story, the words and tears flowed out in anguished waves. I was thirty-seven and feared I might not live a lot longer, that every heartbeat might be my last. Would I be the next to collapse on a run? My kidneys were failing. What about my wife and kids?

Out of that first session, we established that I had to start sharing my anxieties with family and friends who might be only too willing to listen. Up until then, JoAnne and I had decided that we wouldn't tell our kids anything until they were both older and/or we absolutely had to. Dave was twelve, and Amy was ten. My counselor suggested that we should speak with them and be direct and honest.

One evening after dinner, we told them both that we wanted to sit down and have a talk. Our strategy was to make sure that they knew that people in kidney failure could have productive lives and that, while my condition was not to be minimized, it could be managed either by dialysis or transplant. At the time, Gary Coleman, the TV actor, had a successful career despite end-stage kidney failure, managed by dialysis. His health problems were well known. We would approach the matter by telling our kids that I had a condition similar to Gary Coleman's and that, while I would eventually have to go on dialysis or have a transplant, I would be able to carry on and be productive.

Most importantly, we wanted to convey the idea that my life was not in immediate danger.

I began, "Do the two of you know who Gary Coleman is?"

"Yeah," Amy replied without hesitation, "he died, didn't he?"

This wasn't starting out well.

"Ahhh, no. No, Amy, he didn't die. He's on dialysis because his kidneys don't work. In a few years, that will happen to me." We went on to explain that I had a condition that would cause my kidneys to fail but wouldn't constitute an immediate threat to my life because of the dialysis or transplant options. I don't recall discussing the genetic implications at the time. They seemed to accept it as matter-of-factly as we tried to present it. Moreover, we established a line of communication about a situation that would inevitably affect us all.

My counselor had been correct. I noticed reduced anxiety in knowing that we could share this with our kids and the four of us would be able to deal with this as a family. I continued to see him for several months, during which time he took a break from his job and had his transplant. A few years later he became one of the Reading Hospital's lunchtime jocks who I would encounter during my occasional forays onto the hospital's tennis courts. I believe he valued those matches as much as I did.

In late summer of that year, my mother visited us from Florida. One evening she received a call from my brother Ed. He had been admitted to the hospital near his home in Berkeley, CA. His kidneys had failed, and he was going to begin dialysis. Sadly, Ed had ignored my warnings. He had progressed to end-stage kidney failure with no medical management. For at least several years, he had likely been seriously hypertensive. He would later pay a steep price for his own medical negligence.[4]

---

[4] After eleven years on dialysis, Ed received a kidney transplant in 1996. Five years later, he had a heart attack and had bypass surgery. Seven years after that, he had another heart attack, following which a cardiac catheterization was performed, his second. Unfortunately, the dye used in that procedure is toxic to kidneys. His transplant failed, and he returned to dialysis. More cardiac events followed, and he died in 2011 at the age of sixty-one.

Upon hearing Ed's news, my mother, who up to that point was ignorant of my condition, speculated that some of his experiments with pot years earlier had been the likely cause. I knew I needed to disabuse her of that notion.

"Mom," I said, "this is going to happen to me too. The red blood cells and protein that were found in each of our urine tests all those years ago, along with our hearing loss, are part of a genetic condition called Alport syndrome. It had nothing to do with having had measles as kids or a strep infection or any of that stuff. That was all wrong. Those diagnoses had been mistaken."

She was stunned. Now, she would have to deal with the implications of Alport syndrome for her sons. I assured her that Rita had not inherited this condition. That was of some comfort, but the news still hit her hard. I was glad, though, that we had decided some months earlier to be honest and open about this.

By early 1986, almost three years after being told that my kidneys were slowly failing, my blood pressure had crept up to the point that antihypertensive management was indicated. The drug of choice at the time belonged to a class of pharmaceuticals called beta blockers. I was given to understand that effective hypertension control via beta blocker might well reduce my tolerance for exercise.

On a chilly, gray Saturday morning in January, I was about to find out for myself. I dressed for a cold weather run and went out for a short two-miler around town. I may have planned to run a longer distance but cut it short. It was obvious that the pill I had started to take for blood pressure would be hard to swallow in more ways than one. Running was my connection to some feeling of well-being and provided me with the sense that I could still do my part to fight back and resist the inevitable progression of this invisible adversary. I resolved to fight harder.

I also thought about Mickey Mantle. Maybe this was why I found his story so compelling all those years earlier. On some days, when I found it difficult to summon the energy to go out for a run, I thought of Mick. There must have been times he wanted to bag it and not take the field for yet another game due to the pain of his injuries, but he knew his teammates were counting on him and he couldn't let them down.

I had a young family. I had to do everything I could to maximize my chances of having a good outcome after all of this. I had no choice but to lace up my running shoes and go out for my run no matter how crappy I might feel.

After a few months of trying to "run through" my new limitations, I approached my doctor about alternatives. He understood how important running was to me and agreed to let me try clonidine, a centrally acting drug. It would work in my brain to reduce peripheral vascular resistance. I might have experienced better exercise tolerance, but it didn't matter because it made me depressed as hell. Back to the drawing boards. I was then switched to a relatively new class of drug called ACE inhibitors (angiotensin-converting enzymes). But the bottom line was that there was a lot of metabolic dysfunction going on in my body that limited my overall energy and my capacity for exercise. From early 1986 until I received Rita's left kidney four years later, I was increasingly limited in my ability to perform athletically.

In the late summer of 1988, though, I pulled off one of the most ill-advised stunts of my life when I decided to train for and participate in the Green Lane Triathlon. Scott had discovered triathlons a few years earlier. He was a strong bike rider, participated in a few bike races, and only had to add swimming to his training repertoire to become a competitive triathlete. I took an interest in his endeavors and, in the summer of 1988, decided to do enough "cross-training" that perhaps an attempt at a triathlon might be feasible. My reasoning, to whatever meager extent reason had anything to do with it, was that neither biking nor swimming were quite as aerobically taxing as running, at least at the pace I planned. Perhaps by cross-training, I could maintain some level of cardiovascular fitness as my ability to run longer distances waned.

By this time, my serum creatinine level[5] hovered somewhere between three and four. At the time, nephrologists used the inverse of the serum creatinine level to provide the patient with a general measure of their remaining kidney function, so a creatinine level of two meant that you had roughly half of your kidney function (three meant you had a third, etc.). In undoubtedly the greatest example of "don't try this at home" in my life, with somewhere between a third and a quarter of normal kidney function remaining, I joined Scott in entering the Green Lane Triathlon. As tris go, Green Lane would be considered a "sprint" triathlon in today's jargon. The swim was a quarter mile in the Green Lane reservoir, followed by a relatively short fifteen-mile bike ride, and finishing with a five-mile run. I figured I could manage a five-miler, and neither the swim nor bike ride was beyond my capacity, as long as I didn't expect to be competitive. I didn't, and I wasn't.

I got through the swim in the last third of the field and survived the moderately hilly bike ride. But after using my legs for the swim and bike, they just didn't appreciate that I was about to put them through a five-mile run. My body was simply not clearing the metabolites of vigorous exercise well enough to permit sustained activity to the extent required by participating in a triathlon. The cramps were persistent and painful. To fight them off, I ran most of the race with a stride not unlike Chaplin's "little tramp" character. It was a losing battle. I have no idea of my time or place, but suffice it to say, I was easily one of the last finishers. I felt some small degree of gratification, mostly because, despite everything, I gutted it out to the end. However, the implications were obvious. The days of an active lifestyle that I equated with health and well-being and self-identity were over.

As if not to give up completely, I started playing tennis with some of Reading Hospital's lunchtime jocks, but it wasn't the same.

---

5   Serum creatinine refers to a measure of creatinine, a byproduct of muscle and protein metabolism. Most labs report normal creatinine levels between 0.6 and 1.3 milligrams per deciliter of blood as a normal range. Kidney function is considered abnormal when serum creatinine is above this range.

## CHAPTER SEVEN

## *Our Dream Home . . . and Dialysis*

Since my initial finding of elevated creatinine in March 1983, I had semiannual lab work and physical exams to monitor the status of my kidney function and its effect on my overall health. Eventually, the interval between labs was ratcheted down to every three months. In the spring of 1989, my serum creatinine had risen once again, this time to seven. That meant that I had less than 20 percent of normal kidney function. However, it was determined that, since I wasn't feeling a whole lot worse than I had been feeling all along and my blood pressure was stable on medications, I would stay the course and run labs again in three months. That turned out to be the most dubious medical decision we would encounter in this whole process, but for the time being, we would go on with our lives as normally as possible.

In the early winter of the previous year, we had purchased a one-and-a-half-acre lot in a new subdivision that featured trees—lots of them. We would build our dream home. The location offered a sense of privacy without being secluded. We signed a purchase contract, interviewed builders, and chose one. We looked at myriad house plans, selected and modified one, and attended to minutiae, such as style of handles, drawer pulls, hinges on kitchen cabinets, colors, types of siding, and even the location of the house footprint on our leafy lot. To save money, we would paint the interior of the house ourselves. All in the face of my impending kidney failure. Wouldn't anyone?

In addition, I tried to continue to be as physically active as possible and entered Reading Hospital's tennis tournament early that summer. I faced a singles match on a warm afternoon after work in which my opponent and I were even in terms of ability. What I lacked in legitimate tennis skill, I made up for with good court speed, which necessarily meant that I would do a lot of running around. I lost the close first set. The second set was tied midway through when my opponent deftly placed a series of shots to alternating sides of the court. I scrambled to return each one successfully, running the width of the court three times with no respite before he lost the point by missing an easy put-away shot into the net. It was the last point I won for the entire match. I had no reserve energy. My legs resented any attempt at propelling my body any faster than a casual shuffle. By the time I drove home and got out of the car, I could barely walk. My body's ability to process the metabolic waste products of muscle activity was so compromised that my muscle fibers were screaming, *What the hell is wrong with you, Gance? We're being pickled by acids and toxins, and you think you're Jimmy Connors!* Essentially, my body was refusing my athletic demands.

Not long after, with our house about two-thirds complete, our builder advised us that the interior painting and staining could proceed. However, lab results in late July showed that my creatinine had jumped up to eleven. While a kidney transplant was my long-term option, putting off dialysis further was now completely out of the question. I was told in no uncertain terms that I was about to become "very sick, very fast." I would have to go on dialysis until our lives settled down and we could get the transplant scheduled.

I chose peritoneal dialysis over hemodialysis[6] as my best option. In as much as I planned to continue to work and be as active as I could, peritoneal dialysis was a no-brainer. I would perform the procedure myself at home and at work. While it would take about thirty-five minutes four times daily, I would not be tethered to a machine in a dialysis center for hours.

I was admitted to Reading Hospital for insertion of a Tenckhoff catheter into my abdomen, slightly below and about an inch and a half to the right of my navel, to be performed as an outpatient under local anesthesia with sedation. The indwelling part of the Tenckhoff more or less floats in the peritoneal cavity, the highly vascular enclosure in which the body's abdominal organs are suspended. The internal walls of the peritoneum are capillary dense, facilitating osmotic transfer (through the cell walls of the peritoneum) of metabolic waste. After a healing period of about ten days, I would begin my dialysis.

Meanwhile, our house painting project was about to begin. JoAnne and I each arranged to take vacation time to paint the interior. A day or two after the catheter insertion, I walked into the closest Glidden store and placed an order for forty-five gallons of paint in various colors and finishes. The clerk looked at me curiously before commenting, "That's the most paint I've ever sold to anyone at one time!" It failed to occur to me that her exclamation had a slightly ominous tone.

On top of all of that, we had sold our home almost immediately after putting it up for sale, and the closing date was set. We would have to move out before our new home was complete. Fortunately,

---

6  In hemodialysis, blood is pumped out of the body through tubes into a dialysis machine that cleanses it and delivers it back into the body. The access is usually through a shunt in the forearm. Hemodialysis is usually performed in an outpatient dialysis center for three to five hours three times per week. Peritoneal dialysis uses the lining of the abdominal cavity (peritoneum) into which a two-liter bag full of dialysate (a sugar-water type substance) is delivered via tubing connected to a catheter in the lower abdomen, usually four times per day. Each "fluid exchange" takes about thirty-five minutes. It is considered to be more natural than hemodialysis and, with adept planning, allows the patient to continue to work, at least in the kind of office setting in which I worked.

we knew of a young friend who was vacating a very small, furnished apartment nearby and arranged to lease it for the next two months. JoAnne investigated storage units where we could house all our worldly possessions, but there were none to be had. Once again, our friends came through. Scott and Judy Giacobbe and Sue and Steve Horst offered their garages for storage, as did our new neighbors across the street, John and Barbara Volpe. We set the moving date.

As our painting project began, friends made time in their busy schedules to help. A few worked in public schools and were generous in sharing some of their summer break to help us out. Our soon-to-be next-door neighbor, Gerry Chasse, was recently retired and working on his new home with his wife Bonnie. He would amble over, announcing, "I can give you two hours this afternoon." I would hand him a paint roller and a can of paint and assign him a room.

About a week after my dialysis catheter was inserted, but still prior to beginning treatment, I was staining molding when I started to feel nauseous. Actually, I had had the same feeling for a few mornings in a row, but this time it was more noticeable. It finally got bad enough that I opened the brand-new French doors that would eventually lead out to a deck off the back of the house, threw up onto the ground below, closed the doors, cleaned myself up, and resumed staining. I took some comfort that barfing my guts out through our classy new doors was better than hanging my head over the toilet, but, to be sure, this was not a good sign. My body was beginning to become toxified by the waste products building up rapidly in my system. A little later I called my nephrologist and reported on my condition. He told me that I would have to begin dialysis the next morning, a Saturday . . . the day we were scheduled to move out of our old house. Waiting any longer would pose a significant risk to my overall health. The timing could not have been worse.

The next day, shortly after the moving van arrived at our house, JoAnne supervised Dave, Amy, and many of our friends in carrying boxes, furniture, and belongings to their various designated locations as I drove to the dialysis center. There, I was instructed in the thirty-nine-step procedure of introducing two liters of dialysis fluid into my peritoneal space and draining spent fluid. The process required using an IV pole and a set of flexible tubes in the shape of a Y to introduce the two liters of dialysate, a sugar-water like substance, into my peritoneum. In that way, the largely acidic accumulation of metabolic waste from my cells and blood would be drawn into the fluid by osmosis, thus removing toxins from my system. I would perform this new ritual on a four-times-daily basis; each fluid exchange would take approximately thirty-five minutes. At the beginning of each fluid exchange, the "old" dialysis fluid, introduced during the previous exchange, would be drained through the catheter and tubing prior to the introduction of fresh fluid. In that way, I would be purged of enough toxic metabolites to continue some semblance of a normal lifestyle without having to tolerate the two- or three-day buildup of toxins inherent in hemodialysis.

Under the supervision of a very attentive and concerned dialysis nurse, I set up my IV poles, ran the first bag of fluid into my system, and immediately began to feel faint and woozy. I never quite passed out, but I came close. The nurse microwaved a cup of broth for me to sip, and I began to feel better. The sudden release of high levels of bodily toxins from my bloodstream and body cells had caused a relatively abrupt volume change, which manifested itself in a hypotensive (low blood pressure) episode.

Finally, with two liters of dialysis fluid in my peritoneum, multiple boxes of dialysis fluid bags, an IV pole, and dialysis instruction flashcards in tow, I drove to our new home and joined JoAnne, our kids, our friends, and our neighbors, who were busy with ongoing projects. Six hours later, at our rented mini-apartment, I sat down for my first solo fluid exchange, which went off without a hitch. This would be my routine until we could get my transplant scheduled.

Our cramped temporary quarters meant that we had to farm out our kids in alternate shifts. Dave stayed with the family of a school friend during the week and with us on weekends. Amy stayed with us during the week and with Scott and Judy Giacobbe on weekends. Meanwhile, I tried to run at lunch a few times, but with two liters of dialysis fluid sloshing around in my peritoneum, I felt unbalanced and excruciatingly slow. Tennis was less problematic. A doubles match at lunch became my daily exercise routine. That effort, too, resulted in a memorable but painful moment.

We pretty much lived out of suitcases and plastic milk crates in our tiny apartment. One of the milk crates held my athletic gear. Early one dark morning, I grabbed my tennis clothes and hurriedly stuffed them into my duffel bag so I could play at lunch. I was the first of the lunchtime jocks to arrive at the locker room, and I began to change. I reached into my bag for my bikini-type athletic supporter and pulled out a pair of our fourteen-year-old daughter's underpants—pale-pink with lace borders. They had mistakenly been deposited in the wrong milk crate.

I faced a dilemma. Either abandon tennis plans for that day or squeeze into Amy's underwear before any of the guys arrived. Tennis had, for the time being, replaced running as my emotional link to athleticism and health. Not playing even for a day was out of the question. Amy's undies would never be the same, but I managed to don them and hurriedly got into my tennis shorts before anyone else showed up.

We played our doubles match and returned to the locker room, at which point I faced my next dilemma: how to get my shorts and Amy's panties off without anyone noticing, which no doubt would have caused me unending ribbing or resulted in a permanent ban from athletics at Reading Hospital. There was only one way to do it. I would remove my tennis shorts and Amy's undies in one fell swoop. . . . No one would be any the wiser.

This turned out to be easier said than done. In grabbing both articles of clothing at one time and yanking them off, the upper elastic band grabbed onto the port of my Tenckhoff catheter, which was secured in place internally by an integrated grommet and scar tissue that had built up around it. Fortunately, I didn't yank the thing out. The pain was short lived but intense. I let out a muffled but audible grunt. One of the guys asked if I was okay. I managed a tepid assurance that all was well and it was just a leg cramp as I continued to wiggle out of my tennis shorts and Amy's panties, which, after forty-five minutes of tennis on a warm day, were drenched with crotch-perspiration and stretched beyond recognition. Needless to say, Amy never wore them again. Neither did I.

On two occasions, I made excruciatingly painful mistakes in the sequence of accomplishing a fluid exchange. Fortunately, they turned out to have no long-term consequences. Late one Saturday evening, I set up to do my final exchange of the day just before bedtime. At the end of each exchange, I would run a Clorox-type solution into the tubing lines to keep them sterile between exchanges. At the beginning of the next exchange, it was necessary to drain the Clorox into a used IV bag attached to one of the arms of the Y tubing, which would receive the spent, toxified fluid that had dwelt in my peritoneum since the last exchange. This was accomplished by opening and closing several clamps that allowed the Clorox to drain into the bag on the floor. Opening and closing the clamps in the wrong order would mean that I'd get a four-foot line full of Clorox in my peritoneum.

Even though I had accomplished this procedure flawlessly four times daily for two months, I made a mistake, a realization that occurred to me the instant I doubled over in pain as though the heavyweight champ had landed a clean punch to my gut. For a short time, it sent my diaphragm into spasms, forcing shallow, rapid intercostal breathing as the pain brought me to tears. JoAnne was seated on the couch next to me, and I slumped over to lean on her for support. I had the presence of mind to realize that I had no choice but to allow the fresh bag of dialysis fluid to run into my peritoneum and dilute the Clorox. The diaphragm spasms and pain gradually resolved, but it had been a scary experience for both of us. I vowed never to repeat it again.

Repeat it again I did, this time in my office. I worked on Tuesday evenings and, in the process of my dinnertime fluid exchange, made the same mistake. The fact that it was a repeat performance seemed to take the edge off the pain to a small degree. Perhaps my peritoneum had adapted to my stupidity. That my abdominal organs must have been sparkling clean was of little comfort.

Despite those jolting events, peritoneal dialysis served me well. I was able to continue to work, to help with the completion of our new house, and to participate in family activities. There was even a sense of emotional relief. I had come face-to-face with end-stage-kidney failure, the condition I had regarded with dread for six years, and found that it could be managed through the combination of excellent medical care by my nephrologists and dialysis team, by my own obsession with understanding the nature of my illness and its management, and by the presence of a loving and understanding family and supportive friends. Just the same, I looked forward with excitement to my upcoming kidney transplant.

We moved into our new home on September 30. A few weeks later, we threw a party for all our friends, old and new, who had helped us in so many ways. JoAnne made a big pot of chili, and we honored their generosity in sharing their homes, garages, and time. They enabled us to arrive at this day relatively unscathed. In the middle of festivities, I excused myself and went upstairs to our bedroom to perform a fluid exchange, then rejoined our friends for the remainder of the gathering. This was our new normal.

Rita had, by this time, committed to be my donor. In the years since my diagnosis, she had watched my health deteriorate gradually. Her enthusiastic response to my need for a kidney was a function of a confluence of factors that would not come to light for years, but suffice it to say, she looked up to me as her older brother, understood my role as husband and father, and cherished her aunt-niece and -nephew relationship with both Dave and Amy. She was in some ways their wise and understanding older sister, in other ways their trusted friend; moreover, she was fun to be with. By this time, Ed had been on dialysis for four years. Rita did not want our mom to have to see both of her sons living limited lives threatened by renal failure. She offered to give a kidney to whomever of us was the better match. Reet and I had been tissue-matched a few years earlier in anticipation of the transplant and found that we matched on five out of six "antigens." Only identical twins match six of six. Ed indicated that he would continue dialysis, in part because he lived three thousand miles away in Berkeley, CA, but also because, as a regular patient at an outpatient hemodialysis center, he saw patients whose bodies had rejected transplants. Some told personal horror stories about the process. Ed decided he didn't want any part of it.

In early December, JoAnne accompanied Reet and I as we traveled to Hershey Medical Center for an evaluation to determine whether she was medically and psychologically suitable to be a kidney donor. Over the course of a few hours, we were examined and interviewed while the staff reviewed test results that had been performed on each of us in Reading. We were told that Rita would receive a call from the transplant coordinator. We left Hershey optimistic that, within a month or so, one of Rita's kidneys would be nestled in my body.

A few days later she walked into my office and burst into tears. Hershey had called and told her that she would not be a suitable donor because the urine collection system of her kidneys had a structural anomaly that might make them more prone to infection and stones.

I was disappointed but knew that I could go on a transplant waiting list and would likely receive a kidney in twelve to eighteen months. But Rita was devastated, far beyond what I would have anticipated. Years later I would gain further understanding of why she was so distraught.

However, Hershey's transplant coordinator held out a ray of hope. She told Rita that, since Hershey's organ transplantation program was relatively new, we might want to investigate one of the more established and experienced transplant programs in Philadelphia. She then sought out one of my nephrologists for an opinion. He told her that he saw no reason that she couldn't be a donor, and since she had no history of urinary tract infections or stones, neither of us was likely to have problems. We made an appointment at the transplant clinic at the Hospital of the University of Pennsylvania (HUP) where, after another evaluation and review of each of our histories, we were given the green light to proceed. At last, the transplant date was scheduled.

On the afternoon of Sunday, February 18, 1990, JoAnne, Amy, Rita, and I made the ninety-minute drive to the Penn campus in West Philadelphia. After a tedious admission process, Reet and I found ourselves ensconced in our respective rooms on Radvin 7, the HUP transplant floor. Immediately upon being introduced to our new quarters, Amy magically produced cheery banners featuring witty observations about peeing as well as heartfelt good wishes. Rita had made a small poster depicting a happy-looking kidney, strolling from her to me. Dave had contributed some cartoon drawings featuring his alter ego, Calvin, of *Calvin and Hobbes*. To this day, it is likely that no transplant patient's room has ever been decorated with such fine, inspiring art.

On Monday, there were more blood draws to confirm that neither of us had contracted a virus since our last tissue-typing, which would cause a serious and immediate rejection response. The results were negative; all systems were *go*.

That night, JoAnne and my mom, who had flown up from Florida, stayed with some college friends of ours who lived just outside of Philadelphia. Amy and Dave also spent the night at the homes of friends and went to school the next morning. We wanted to keep their lives as ordinary as possible on this decidedly extraordinary day.

At six o'clock Tuesday morning, a nurse came into my room to tell me that Rita was about to be transported to the operating room to begin the process of prepping her for the open nephrectomy, during which her surgeon would retrieve her left kidney. I had just awoken from a terrific night's sleep, which I attributed to the peace of mind brought on by the assurance that we—me, the medical teams working on my behalf, my family, and above all, Rita—were as prepared as humanly possible. It was a comforting thought. I also had to consider that 50 mg of Benadryl at bedtime the night before had something to do with my restful night. But, beyond that, the sense of peace, the sense that, in the words of fourteenth-century Christian mystic Julian of Norwich, "All will be well, and all will be well, and all manner of thing will be well," was beyond anything I could have expected. I was being held, and I knew it.

I walked over to Rita's room and gave her a hug. Words seemed inadequate to express my gratitude. We had anticipated this moment for almost seven years. I wanted to think that her previous experience with surgeries had prepared her emotionally for this, but I'm not sure anything could have. She seemed pensive but resolute. I told her that our dad would have been proud. In truth, he hated medical situations and would have been terrified at the thought of what was about to transpire. I kissed her on the forehead, told her I loved her, and went back to my room to await my ride to the operating room, which would follow hers by about an hour.

My last presurgery task was to drain my overnight dialysis fluid without replacing it. Not much later, I was brought to the OR. As I was being transferred to the operating table, I told the surgical team that I was beginning to feel a bit woozy and that, as a result of my overnight dialysis, I was a little "dry." Within seconds, they had set up an IV. I felt better almost immediately. By this time, Rita's nephrectomy was underway in an adjoining OR. My surgeon approached and told me that all was proceeding well and that my surgery would begin momentarily.

Twenty-five years had passed since the first indication of a kidney abnormality arose during a physical exam for a summer job. I could not then have imagined the journey that lay before me, my family, and Rita. It had come down to this moment. Another IV was placed to begin the anesthesia. In the second or two of suspended reality that preceded unconsciousness, I briefly pondered . . . I wonder . . . when I awake with my new kidney . . . perhaps a fanfare . . . maybe even a symphony . . .

Rita's poster showing her happy-looking kidney strolling from her to me.

# PART II

CHAPTER EIGHT

## *My Second Life*

In 1990 the standard of care for the immediate postoperative hospitalization period following kidney transplant required six to seven days of close monitoring for signs of organ rejection or other complications. This included daily blood draws for kidney function measures.

On post-transplant, day one, the chief nephrologist walked into my room with a resident physician in tow. As he reviewed my case, I heard him say "creatinine 1.4." I interrupted, with no small degree of incredulity in my voice, "1.4! ME?" My creatinine had not been that low in almost ten years. I thought he must have been referring to another patient. He smiled, briefly acknowledging to the resident, and to me, the laboratory-confirmed miracle he beheld before matter-of-factly resuming his review of my case.

That morning, I had gingerly gotten out of bed with the help of a nurse. The next day, I was allowed to get out of bed on my own with a nurse observing. My incision was still a little tender, and I had some anxiety concerning the realization that my sister's kidney was simply stitched to my ureter, a vein, and an artery not far underneath the crescent-shaped incision in my lower left abdomen. I thought about Mick once again. I resolved to get up and get moving, just like my baseball idol would have all those years earlier. What I didn't know then was that, five years later, Mick would have his own transplant story. Sadly, it would not have a positive outcome.

Over the next few days, I began walking around the transplant floor, always stopping by to check on Rita. She was in a lot of pain and experiencing some nausea that would take a few days to resolve. She would wave in acknowledgment but wasn't exactly up for a long visit.

From the window in my room, I was able to look down on Franklin Field, the University of Pennsylvania stadium. I could see a corner of the red-composite running track around the football field and imagined myself running again, a goal whose validity was confirmed by a brochure on a patient bulletin-board inviting transplant recipients to participate in the US Transplant Games. My doctors had told me that I would have few physical limitations after my transplant, but I still had my doubts. After all, this was serious surgery. The Transplant Games brochure banished those doubts once and for all.

The US Transplant Games are Olympic-type events for organ recipients, held every two years. I would find out later that there were World Transplant Games held in the intervening years. The 1990 US games would be held later that year in Indianapolis. With a little imagination, I envisioned the transplant floor's two long parallel hallways, connected at either end by short connector halls, as a running track. Assuming the floor tiles were twelve-inch square standard issue, it was only a matter of counting the tiles on one of the long and short hallways and applying simple math.

At one point, Rita saw me walking slowly past her room, my head down and concentrating on the repetitive tiles in front of me. Upon completing my circuit, I stopped into her room, proclaiming that nine laps around constituted a mile! Despite her pain and finally emerging from a miserable few days of post-anesthesia nausea, she beamed at the miracle she had made possible. For each of my last three days of hospitalization, I did a brisk mile walk after breakfast, one after lunch and one after dinner. I found myself looking forward to the little aerobic challenge I had designed. Resident physicians began to refer to me as the "transplant poster boy."

I felt great. While dialysis patients generally feel well enough to function and, in my case, well enough to continue to work full time, I had been advised that, once I had a transplant, I would appreciate how fatigued I had felt on dialysis and for several years before as my kidneys gradually failed. That prediction turned out to be spot-on.

Rita was discharged on Friday, post-surgery, day three, still in some pain but eager to get out of the hospital. She spent several weeks recuperating at our house under the care of JoAnne and my mother. Then, one-week post-op, I walked out of the hospital of the University of Pennsylvania with Rita's left kidney nestled in my left pelvic recess. In celebration of the occasion, JoAnne came up with an announcement similar to those sent to friends and family upon the birth of a child. A clever drawing of a stork, carrying a kidney suspended in a sling hanging from its beak, was flanked top and bottom with the exclamation, "It's a kidney . . . we couldn't pee happier." She mailed it to friends and relatives near and far. Hallmark couldn't have done better.

After arriving home and grilling a celebratory steak for dinner, I took my first post-transplant home-cooked bite and exclaimed, "Is this a particularly good steak, or does steak always taste as good as this"?

JoAnne answered with some delight that this was a good steak, but yes, generally, steaks do taste like this. I hadn't noticed that the metabolic changes accompanying kidney failure and dialysis had altered my taste perception. It was certainly back to normal now.

That evening, my running buddy, Scott, stopped over to check me out. I was squatting down by the fireplace, getting a blaze started, as he walked into our family room. He looked at me and exclaimed, "Bobby! You look amazing." What he was really saying in not so many words was "You looked like hell for so long. . . . It's incredible to see you looking so healthy so soon." Through the pain, Rita smiled ear to ear as she lay on the couch.

Two weeks post-op, I went back to work part-time, then full time a few weeks later, feeling more energy than I had in years. As my kidneys were failing, and during my time on dialysis, I would have to take a short rest between patients to gather the mental energy for the next encounter. Upon returning to work, I immediately noticed that I could see patient after patient without having to sit for a few minutes of recovery after each one. A month later I resumed lunchtime tennis. But tennis was, for me, a temporary substitute for running. While it was more fun and had a social element, it lacked the intense and sustained aerobic challenge offered by running. I held out hope that I would be able to continue to run after my transplant.

A week after my post-transplant tennis debut, I went for a lunchtime run, a two-mile jog around a nearby track on a sunny early spring day. I had a heightened awareness of Rita's precious kidney miraculously making the whole thing possible. After the run, I returned to the locker room with a sense of awe—the physiologic limitations that had gradually conspired to deprive me of the one physical activity that I most associated with health, vigor, and life itself had vanished thanks to my sister's selfless gift. My second life was beginning to take shape.

CHAPTER NINE

## *The Best of Times, the Worst of Times*

The summer of 1990 was the first in many years in which I had a normally functioning kidney in my body. We spent a week in Wilmington, NC, visiting JoAnne's brother Kim and his wife Jeri. In those days, vacations meant spending long days on the beach, swimming, body surfing, and, even in my newly immunosuppressed state, soaking up sun. Then, on the way back to PA, we stopped in Williamsburg and Busch Gardens, VA. That level of activity would have been impossible for me just a short time earlier.

After arriving back home in mid-August, I began to notice some swelling in my ankles and had some days in which I generally felt fatigued. A visit to the transplant clinic at Penn failed to reveal anything of concern, but within two weeks, the swelling, which had been confined to my legs and ankles at day's end, was up in my face in the morning, suggesting that I was not peeing out fluid sufficiently. JoAnne accompanied me on another visit to Penn.

This time, lab results suggested that my kidney function had begun to deteriorate. The doctor decided to perform a kidney biopsy. After we waited around for about an hour, the results came back. I was experiencing moderate organ rejection. I had known that organ rejection was a possibility all along, but it was still a punch in the gut—for both of us.

It was explained that I would need to be admitted immediately for treatment, which would consist of daily IV infusions of an antirejection drug for ten days. I was assured that this was my best chance of beating back components of my immune system that had recognized Rita's precious gift as an intruder and were attacking it. The transplant nephrologist was straightforward.

"We're giving you our best shot. We want to see you keep this kidney for twenty years." He further explained that evidence was beginning to show that the more aggressively rejection episodes were treated, the less chance one would recur and the longer I would be likely to keep my new kidney. Implied was the suggestion that after my body was subjected to this treatment, it wouldn't dare act up again.

While waiting to be admitted, I found a phone and called Rita, faced with the task of telling her that her kidney was in danger of being rejected by my body. Through tears on both ends of the line, I expressed my deep and profound gratitude and promised to do whatever it took to fight this off. "I'd do it all again in a minute if I could" was her reply. I recalled the words John's Gospel attributes to Jesus: "No one has greater love than this, to lay down one's life for one's friend." Or brother.

The field of transplant medicine was still in relative infancy in the late summer of 1990. The world's first kidney transplant was performed thirty-six years earlier, in 1954. In that case, the living donor and the recipient were identical twins. That meant that they were identical genetically, and there would be little or no likelihood of rejection. It was not until 1983, with the approval of cyclosporine as the primary antirejection drug, that transplantation became a viable option for more and more patients with organ system failure. The cyclosporine era opened the possibility of much longer "graft survival" in nongenetically identical donor/recipient matches. Pre-op tests for genetic compatibility showed that Rita and I matched on five out of six antigens (proteins on cells that help the body identify its own tissue versus foreign tissue), about as close as we could get without being identical twins. Despite that, and despite state-of-the-art immunosuppressive management,

I still went into rejection. At the time, the likelihood of a rejection episode in the first six months post-transplant was 80 percent (it is now much lower), so I was not alone. For that reason, protocols for managing organ rejection had been developed. The specialists at Penn chose to treat my rejection episode with OKT-3. Among medical staffers, OKT-3 was referred to as "mouse serum." Some elaboration is in order.

Of the many kinds of white blood cells that make up the human immune system, T cells, in particular T-3 cells, have the most relevance to the field of immunosuppression management in organ transplants. Somewhere along the way, thankfully, prior to August 1990, researchers had the bright idea of injecting human T-3 cells into mice. The mice obliged by producing T-3 lymphocytes, yet another kind of immune system cell that would attack the patient's T-3 cells, which, in case of active rejection, were going hog wild attacking the transplanted organ. I had been assured that the OKT-3 I would be given had been produced synthetically and had not been drawn from mice. At that point, I wouldn't have objected if it had come from rats at the city dump.

It worked . . . but the side effects were brutal. Fortunately, they were temporary. In essence, there was a T-cell war going on in my body. The destruction of my rogue T-cells by the injected rodent-inspired crusaders set off an ugly chain reaction that expressed itself in severe flu symptoms. Some patients respond even more catastrophically, as was made clear to me when a nurse wheeled a "crash cart" into my room the evening in which I was to receive my first injection. It remained there for ten days. Thankfully, I didn't "crash." Instead, I ran high fevers (105), I had severe chills and night sweats (they persisted for months), I had yellow goop in my eyes, which caked at the corners, and my blood pressure rose. At one point, my hands and fingers were so swollen that JoAnne had to feed me, although I didn't feel like eating much. I learned that the nursing staff had an even better name than "mouse serum" for OKT-3. In typical nurse humor, OKT-3 was referred to as "shake and bake" on the Penn transplant floor. Eventually, my creatinine levels began to come down. I had survived my ten days of treatment. My rejection episode had been arrested.

Yet it was not all misery. As is often the case, my family's great wit came to the fore in gallows humor appropriate for the occasion. JoAnne brought in cartoon drawings by Rita and Dave and displayed them prominently in my room. Rita's was an accurate depiction of the cartoon cat-and-mouse Tom and Jerry, with Tom hiding a mallet behind his back, about to smash little Jerry to mush. Her caption read, "How to Make Mouse Serum," something to seriously ponder as the stuff coursed through my body. Dave, presaging a career in pharmaceutical research, drew a peeved Calvin, of the *Calvin and Hobbes* comic strip, wearing a pissed-off glare. The caption read, "T-cells . . . can't live with 'em, can't live without 'em," which brought comments from medical staff about its simple eloquence in expressing a sobering reality.

Early on, I was feeling well enough to watch a football game on TV. It was the first weekend of the NFL season, and the Sunday night televised game was Giants versus Eagles. Each bed had six-inch TVs suspended on a boom that could easily be brought into place so it was possible to watch without disturbing my roommate who, undoubtedly, was an Eagles fan, Philadelphia being the ultimate lion's den from a Giants fan's point of view. Through goopy eyes, in my fevered, semidelirious state, I watched Bill Parcells's Giants beat loudmouth Buddy Ryan's Eagles by one touchdown. It turned out to be an omen for both the Giants and for me. I recovered from my rejection episode, and the Giants went on to win the Super Bowl that season.

Once my ten days of IV treatment was over, I began to feel better and was given permission to get up, walk around, and even go outside. One day JoAnne and I went for a walk around the Penn campus. On the way back to my room, we ended up on a crowded elevator that suddenly shot up to the roof, something to do with the hospital's response to an airlift landing on their helipad. Here I was, still substantially immunosuppressed, stuck on a crowded elevator full of people in various degrees of good or ill health, inhaling and exhaling who-knows-what. Somehow, I managed not to come down with any serious airborne infection, but the situation illustrated the concerns we would have as my immune system recovered from the dual assaults of the rejection and the treatment.

I was released two weeks after I was admitted, rejection controlled but still heavily immunosuppressed. I was placed on a regimen of a new class of antiviral drugs to try to ward off any opportunistic viruses that might come my way. I was out of work for a full month but began running again as soon as I felt some strength returning. Then, in mid-November, I was back at Penn again, this time for a week to treat a urinary tract infection that, thanks to my immunosuppressed state, had crossed over into my bloodstream. IV antibiotics knocked that back, and I was home for Thanksgiving. It had been a roller-coaster fall.

In early December JoAnne, Amy, and I drove to Philadelphia to see one of the early touring productions of *Les Misérables*. Anyone who has ever seen that play knows the emotional powerhouse presented by the compelling, heroic story and gorgeous musical score. The year had been full of challenges for us, and, for the most part, we had held our emotions in check to deal with those challenges as they arose. That night, we watched and listened through tears for two-thirds of the production, sobbed at the stirring finale, and left the theater as emotional, wet noodles. The year 1990 had indeed been quite a year.

We celebrated a very merry and gratitude-filled Christmas, but a day or two later, I noticed some symptoms that suggested that another UTI had reared its head. This was becoming somewhat discouraging. We drove back down to Philadelphia again so I could be admitted to HUP for the fourth time in 1990. I sat in the front seat as JoAnne drove. I looked over at her.

"You didn't sign up for this, did you? Maybe you should have picked a healthier husband."

She glanced over at me as if to tell me I must be out of my mind. How could I *possibly* think that? It was obvious that she had taken "in sickness and in health" very seriously and could not imagine that I would even think such a thing. We would go through this together. How humbling to think that I was the recipient of such magnanimous and undeserved love. Throughout this complete process, JoAnne was a rock.

Because we had identified this infection early, the docs knocked it back quickly, and I was home again for New Years. A low dose of a maintenance antibiotic was prescribed to prevent recurrence.

Thus, 1991 began with the promise of full health for the first time in many years.

Proud of her kidney! Rita and I celebrating "Kidney Day" plus one year.

CHAPTER TEN

## *"I Have Finished the Race"*

During my peak running years, 1979-1985, the "crown jewel" event for Scott, myself, and several of our running buddies was the Philadelphia Distance Run (PDR), a mid-September half-marathon (13.1 miles) that traversed the streets of Philly's historic district and Fairmont Park. While Scott's injuries occasionally prevented him from running Philly, I ran it six years in a row and came to view it as a testimony to my health and dedication to fitness, especially as my kidney function began its slow downward progression. I reasoned that, as long as I could run the PDR, I would be holding decline into kidney failure at bay. But by September 1986, the blood pressure medication I had started taking earlier that year had reduced my tolerance for exercise. Short runs now became labored, and the kind of distance training required to run a half-marathon was beyond my capability. It was hard to visualize a time in the future when I would once again have the upper hand.

Fast-forward to that sunny February day in 1990 as I gazed out my seventh-floor window at HUP less than twenty-four hours after my transplant. Returning to the PDR now became my goal.

On a brilliant late-summer Sunday a year and a half later, I made an emotional return to the Philadelphia Distance Run, accompanied by JoAnne, Amy, and Rita, my support crew and cheering section. Scott Giacobbe and John Ruth, each of whom had plied the roads of western

Berks County with me and thought nothing of spending a pleasant Sunday morning running 13.1 miles, ran along with me. My overall time was slower than it had been when I was in top running form. It mattered little. I was back in the race that had come to symbolize my determination to live an active and healthy lifestyle. It was deeply rewarding, even triumphant, rendered more so because it took place in the shadow of the hospital where the restoration of my health had begun.

I returned to Philly four years later to run with Scott and his son, Dan, who lived and worked in center city Philadelphia not far from the streets we would be running through. There had been a time when I thought I would run the PDR as a celebration of life and health every year for as long as I could put one foot in front of another. But I sensed that "to everything there is a season." For me, the season for running the Philadelphia Distance Run was over.

Instead, I would focus on the US and World Transplant Games. As it turned out, my rejection episode prevented me from even considering participation the year of my transplant, but by the time the next US Transplant Games rolled around in 1992, I was geared up for them. From 1992 through 2000, I attended the US Games five times and the World Games twice. For the most part, I competed in running events; the shortest were 400-meter track races, the longest five-kilometer (3.1-mile) races, both track and road. I also competed in bike races on two occasions. While I had a great deal of success competitively, the transplant games were about much more than athletic competition.

Some of the participants were children who, due to congenital anomalies or early-onset disease, had required organ transplants at a very early age. Often, they faced severe growth restrictions due to the side effects imposed by the corticosteroids required to suppress organ rejection. Yet they were cheered on with every step they ran, every stroke they swam, and every ball they tossed. Their adult counterparts, the athletes at the back of the pack on the racetrack, in the pool, or on the bikes, were cheered on loudly by the crowds witnessing their determination. All of us had faced life-threatening situations; we owed our lives to the selfless generosity of others. The Transplant Games were the ultimate celebration of life. There were no losers.

Some participants had already had several transplants either because of unusual hereditary conditions or, ironically, because some antirejection drugs in use at the time were toxic to kidneys. Those who required high levels of that drug to prevent rejection of a transplanted heart or liver might then be faced with kidney failure and require another transplant sometime down the road. We met diabetics whose kidneys failed due to their underlying disease. While transplants availed them of a normally functioning kidney for a time, those transplanted kidneys would eventually fail because their diabetes would eventually destroy the new kidney. Participating in the games was the perfect antidote for self-pity.

Like the Olympics, the Transplant Games featured opening and closing ceremonies where regional teams of athletes gathered on the field as loved ones and other spectators cheered from the stands. On these occasions, I would find myself lining up on the field with hundreds of individuals, each of whom would have likely been dead or tethered to dialysis had it not been for the courageous decision by someone else, whether a family member, acquaintance, friend, or a stranger's donation of the organs to a loved one, made at times of unspeakable grief. We were living testimonies to the love, selflessness, and courage of others. To a person, we shared a deep sense of humility and gratitude, emotions not lost on those in the stands who were there to support us.

There were poignant moments but also times of great fun. At the World Games in Vancouver in 1993, JoAnne and I attended a criterium bike race. The cyclists would ride multiple laps of a one-mile course. We positioned ourselves along with a few hundred spectators, some of whom were teammates of the participants. We happened to be seated near members of the Italian team. If Italians are known for their fun spirit and zest for life, these folks didn't disappoint. Every time one of their riders would pass by, they would ring bells and sing "Alle-Alle" (Go-Go) in boisterous unison. Those of us nearby couldn't help but join in. Whether or not their singing inspired any teammates to victory was inconsequential. The moment captured the "great-to-be-alive" spirit of the games.

Two years later, the World Games were held in Manchester, England. One evening at a noisy pub where participants had gathered to celebrate, JoAnne, Rita, Dave, Amy, and I found ourselves seated at a table across from some folks from Team Sverige (Sweden). We swapped a few transplant stories, but two things stand out in my mind from that encounter. The Swedes were familiar with American culture, history, and politics. Reciprocally speaking, we Yanks were pretty much ignorant of theirs. One of them observed that US influences were so strong in all Western cultures that they couldn't help but be well versed in such matters. It was said not so much as a complaint but as a statement of fact. That we were holding this discussion in English, in which they were quite fluent, confirmed their point.

All of us were wearing team T-shirts. I sported my Team Philadelphia shirt from the 1992 US Games, and one of our new Swedish friends wore a white, blue, and yellow 1995 World Games shirt with SVERIGE emblazoned on it. There in the middle of a hot, noisy, crowded pub, we vigorously tore off our shirts and traded them, each of us gladly ignoring the foreign sweat and armpit odor permeating our damp apparel. While in the interest of downsizing my wardrobe, I have jettisoned many old running and transplant games T-shirts, but I still have that one and wear it occasionally, often invoking the curious query, "Where the hell is SVERIGE?"

The majority of transplant athletes at the games had received their new kidneys, hearts, livers, or lungs from victims of tragedy or sudden catastrophic illness. In a particularly poignant moment that occurred during the opening ceremonies of the 1992 US Games in Los Angeles, a father gave a brief speech honoring his son, Stewart, who had been an organ donor after his tragic death. As he neared the end of his talk, he looked resolutely at the crowd in the bleachers, then up at the sky, and cried, "Yay, Stewart!"—raising a fist into the air in an attempt to defy his own considerable grief. Everyone joined his cheer for Stewart and, by proxy, for other organ donors who had made this celebration possible. It was, as I recall, the only involvement of donor families at the games that year. Over the course of my participation, donor families gradually became woven into the fabric of the event. Their presence led to the most memorable moment of the games in which I participated. It came, appropriately enough, shortly after my last event in my last games.

The 2000 US Transplant Games were held at the Disney Wide World of Sports Complex in Orlando. On the last day of competition, I participated in a criterium bike race: twelve laps around a one-mile course. During the race, there were several age groups on the course at one time, and after a few laps, I found myself even with another rider for the rest of the race. We alternated "drafting" each other for a few laps as a way to conserve energy. After crossing the finish line, I secured my bike and sought out my fellow competitor to exchange the usual post-race congratulations and introduce myself. I found him engaged in a conversation with an attractive couple in their mid-forties. As we shook hands, I noticed a picture of a teenage girl pinned to the front of his bike jersey. He saw that it had grabbed my attention.

"I'm a heart transplant recipient," he explained, "and she was my donor."

I felt as though I was gazing at the image of a saint. He then gestured toward the couple. "And these are her parents."

I'm not sure what I said. Whatever I did say was inadequate. Maybe I hugged them. I hope I did. The transition from death to life, the core of the Christian tradition, was on display right before my eyes, made possible by a completely selfless act performed in a moment of immense personal grief.

Since each of us had placed either first, second, or third in our respective age group, my fellow cyclist and I had been advised to hang around for the medal ceremony. As in the Olympics, when your name was called, you approached and took your place on the gold, silver, or bronze podium. A volunteer would hang a medal around your neck. When my new friend's name was announced, he took his position. Then, the couple with whom he had been speaking stepped forward and placed his medal around him. It rested on his chest as their daughter's heart beat strongly inside. Through tears, the three shared a hug. I knew I was witnessing something deeply sacred. It was a God moment.

At one time, I thought I would participate in the Transplant Games for as long as I could move a muscle. Our family had planned vacations around them. Both JoAnne and I valued the camaraderie of new friends with whom we shared a unique bond. But the 2,500-year-old wisdom of Ecclesiastes[7] would once again apply. While I enjoyed the competition, we knew that the 2000 Transplant Games would be my last.

Our lives had changed. After graduating from college in 1998, Amy spent a year volunteering with a Catholic organization in Tecolote, Mexico, a dirt-poor town about twenty miles south of Tijuana. She then returned to Mexico in 2002, this time to Mexico City, where she would live for the next six years. Dave had moved to Wilmington, NC, joining JoAnne's sister and brother and families who had relocated there from Upstate New York several years earlier. My mom and her husband, Jim White, continued their active lifestyle in Florida. We had family obligations and other travel interests that would consume our limited vacation time.

There had been a time when I could not have imagined that I would regain the vigor, energy, and spirit to once again participate in the kind of activities that had become so essential to my sense of identity. I enjoyed, even relished, every step I ran, every mile I rode, aware that I had been the undeserving recipient of my courageous little sister's selfless gift. But by the time the 2000 US Transplant Games were over, I knew that I had run the good race, as Paul deftly phrased it. Clearly, the seasons of the Philadelphia Distance Run and the Transplant Games were over.

---

7    Ecclesiastes 3, 1-8.

Rita and I after the Philadelphia Distance Run, September 1991

Myself, Mike Pollard, kidney transplant, England, and Chris Chiarello, kidney/pancreas transplant, US, 1995 World Transplant Games, Manchester, England

CHAPTER ELEVEN

## *Another God Moment*

Almost as soon as I first got out of bed after my transplant, I felt compelled to pay Rita's gift forward by any means possible. At the time, there were about 25,000 Americans on waiting lists for kidney, liver, and heart transplants. According to the United Network for Organ Sharing, an average of eight people would die every day waiting for a suitable organ to become available. Those numbers have since risen exponentially. If my little sister hadn't been willing and able to donate a kidney when I needed one, I would have waited about a year to receive a cadaver kidney.[8] I became acutely aware that I had been afforded the chance to live a life I had, at one time, never thought possible and felt called to loudly and publicly proclaim the need for people to consider organ donation.

I focused on two ways I could effectively express my gratitude to Rita: 1. I vowed to take care of myself physically the best way I knew how, through an active lifestyle, dietary vigilance, and obsessive attention to my medication regimen, and 2. I would pay Rita's gift forward by educating the public about the critical need for organ donation.

As it happened, I was part of a dialysis support group that gradually morphed into a transplant group. From that organization, the Berks County Coalition for Organ and Tissue Donation emerged. Our

---

8   As of late 2024, the wait was about five years.

mission was to engage in activities that might help to educate the public about the need to increase the number of donated organs. This included working with media outlets in the city of Reading and Berks County to generate newspaper articles about local individuals whose lives had been saved by organ transplants. We also ran TV/radio spots and participated in seminars for healthcare professionals. We even worked with the local minor league baseball team, the Reading Phillies, to hold an annual organ donor ceremony before one of the team's games. We marched in a few local Halloween parades, proudly carrying an organ donor banner and handing out organ donor cards and candy.

Public speaking was the type of activity we engaged in most often. We hoped to convince more people to sign and carry an organ donor card, to designate themselves as organ donors on their driver's licenses, and, most importantly, to discuss the matter with family members. Our audiences were civic and church groups and hospital in-services for nurses and other medical staff members. In the process, I realized that just telling my story was inadequate for our purposes. To educate the public about organ donation, both sides of the transplant equation, donor and recipient, had to be heard. Several people in the donor family community joined our group and agreed to speak about their experiences. They had lived through tragic circumstances that claimed the lives of loved ones and found themselves faced with the decision about organ donation at times of unspeakable grief. The donor family representative who accompanied me most often was a pleasant, straightforward lady by the name of Janet Hivner. Our audiences invariably found her story riveting.

Janet's thirty-three-year-old son, Dan, was an engineer, married, healthy, and the father of two small children. He worked out of the Reading, PA, office of a German engineering firm that had sent him to Bangkok, Thailand, to consult on a project and paid for his wife to accompany him. One evening, they went out for a drink to celebrate her birthday. The bars were closed, but they found a speakeasy and sat next to a couple of American GIs. Unbeknown to Dan and his wife, he was about to be the target of a robbery attempt. One of them spiked his drink. The idea, evidently, was to make him lightheaded and possibly faint, at which point they would lift his wallet. As Janet would later tell, although a big, robust fellow, Dan was notoriously poor at holding his liquor. Instead of becoming woozy, he crashed to the floor.

An ambulance was called. Dan was taken to a hospital, where he was put on life support. After some examinations and tests, his wife was told that he was brain-dead and that nothing could be done to save his life. Amid her hysteria, she had the presence of mind to call Janet back in the US. Janet contacted Dan's employer, who immediately sent a medical jet to Bangkok to fly Dan back to Reading on life support, accompanied by his wife. The crew called ahead to the Reading Hospital and Medical Center, appraising them of the situation. Once he arrived at the hospital, he was admitted to intensive care, where a battery of neurologic examinations and tests to determine brain function were administered.

Janet felt confident that the diagnosis in Bangkok had been wrong and that medical care in the US would yield a more positive prognosis. Instead, the conclusion reached by the Bangkok doctors was tragically confirmed. At age thirty-three, Dan Hivner was brain-dead, with no hope of recovery. His family was told that their only option was to remove him from life support. The question they now confronted was whether they would consider donating his organs for transplant before doing so.

Dan's wife deferred the decision to Janet. She agreed. While Dan's critical life functions were maintained, various tests were administered to determine the suitability of his organs for donation. He was then wheeled to an operating room, where teams of surgeons sent by transplant centers in the region removed his kidneys, liver, corneas, and heart. I have been told by operating room nurses that the removal of the heart during organ procurement is among the most reverential of any they experience. Until that moment, monitors beep with every heartbeat, other monitors record critical functions such as pulse, blood pressure, and oxygen saturation, and a ventilator performs every inhalation and exhalation. The heart is the last organ to be removed, after which the monitors go silent and the usual frenetic activity of the OR tapers to a soft hush, the staff aware that they have been instrumental in the termination of one life and the passing on of that life to others. At a time of personal tragedy, Janet Hivner found comfort in the knowledge that her son's death had yielded life for others. She was only too happy to honor him by telling his story.

On a Sunday morning in 2005, Janet and I were speaking to a woman's group at a Lutheran Church in Fleetwood, PA, a small town about twenty miles northeast of Reading. As members of the congregation assembled, I recognized a familiar face. Donna was a radiologic technologist at Reading Hospital and one of Rita's coworkers. We acknowledged each other from across the room as she took her seat.

By this time, Janet and I had developed a tried-and-true routine. I began by briefly telling my story, with emphasis on Rita's decision to donate her kidney and on the impact of that decision on my life and on the lives of my family. Then I showed a professionally produced video of the Transplant Games, featuring vigorous and healthy-looking transplant recipients engaged in athletic activities at various levels of proficiency, each enjoying and maximizing their second chance at life. Emphasizing that the real story was that of the donor and donor family, I then introduced Janet.

She was well into her presentation when I noticed that Donna was particularly moved. After Janet finished and we fielded questions, I approached Donna.

"I remember him," she told me. "I gave him his last hug." She went on to explain that she was part of the team performing imaging studies that were included in the process of determining whether Dan's organs were viable for transplantation. As Dan was about to be wheeled to the operating room, she stopped to give him one final human embrace.

By this time, tears were streaming down her face. I told her that I wanted to introduce her to Janet, who was engaged in conversation with some of the audience members as the assembly was breaking up.

"Donna," I said, "you need to meet Janet."

She was hesitant. "I don't think I can."

"Yes, yes, you can," I assured her and led her over to Janet.

"Janet, this is Donna. Donna is a radiology tech at Reading Hospital," I said, taking a step back.

Then, this kind, young woman approached Janet and sobbed. "I remember your son. I gave him his last hug."

Janet reached out to Donna with a smile spread across her face. They embraced. Janet was moved and gratified that, in the middle of the busy pace of hospital medicine, as her son was about to leave this world, someone had given Dan the hug that she, herself, couldn't. Once again, as in Orlando five years before, I had the impression that I was witnessing something sacred. Dan Hivner's story had come full circle back to Janet. It was another God moment.

CHAPTER TWELVE

## *The Letter*

When I returned home from work on the afternoon of Friday, April 26, 2004, there was a letter from Rita addressed to JoAnne and me. Both the letter and the envelope had been written in Reet's unmistakable handwriting. To say that receiving a letter from my sister was unusual would be an understatement. She lived twenty minutes away by car, worked close to my office, and saw us several times every month. Yet I had a strong idea what the general content would be. At the age of forty-eight, Rita was coming out. She was announcing that she was a lesbian. It was a great surprise to no one.

Rita had never married. Ann had been her close friend and companion for twenty years. They did practically everything together, including vacations, which included yearly visits to my mom. They lived separately, each in her own home, and participated in the life of their Catholic parish in Reading. JoAnne and I had suspected that perhaps they were a couple. However, Rita had a privacy shield that she guarded carefully. There were places where I never felt it was appropriate to venture. Her sexuality was one of them.

In the letter, she told us that she and Ann had been partners all along, but since they could never be affirmed as a "couple," their relationship had eventually become constrained. We later found out that Reet had wanted to "come out" for several years, but Ann had resisted. Now Rita had met another woman, Melissa, with whom she confided. They had become very close, were now a couple, and Melissa was divorcing her emotionally abusive husband and moving in with Rita. We had met Melissa a few times over the past year and were seeing less and less of Ann. It was with Melissa's support that she was making this revelation.

It was the letter's last sentence, though, that spoke volumes. Reet wrote that she would understand if we wanted to cut off our relationship and have no further interactions. On the one hand, I wondered how she could ever think that we would have no more to do with her; on the other hand, I knew that in less enlightened times, I might have had some disparaging things to say about homosexuality. Perhaps she felt I still harbored those feelings.

As it happened, JoAnne and I had plans to go over to Rita's house for dinner the following Sunday. I called her right away to reassure her that 1. We loved her, and 2. We'd be over for dinner Sunday as previously arranged. We would talk then. This was not the type of conversation I wanted to have over the phone.

Since Rita's recovery from spinal fusion surgery a little over a year earlier, JoAnne and I had observed that she seemed depressed. The privacy shield was very much in place, but at some point, not long before receiving the letter, I asked if she was okay. She answered, not by denying a problem but by indicating that she was dealing with it. I had no choice but to acknowledge her reply and asked her to let me know if I could help in any way. We left it at that. Now it was out in the open. I felt a deep sense of gratitude that none of us would be burdened with carrying this secret any longer.

On Sunday, the drive to Rita's house was quiet. JoAnne and I were each caught up in our own thoughts, but each of us knew that, more than anything, we needed to reassure Reet that she was loved. When we arrived, a fleeting moment of awkwardness disappeared in a hug. I decided, though, to put forward one question and resolved that, whatever Rita's answer, I would accept it.

"Reet, the only thing I feel bad about is that you were there for me, but, by not knowing, I couldn't be supportive of you."

Her reply was simple and straightforward: "It just wasn't time, Bob. It just wasn't time." To argue the issue would have been self-centered on my part. This was clearly a time for listening, understanding, and beginning to appreciate what she had been going through.

Over dinner, Reet revealed that our mom and dad had confronted her about her sexuality many years earlier, when she was in her late teens. Our parents were raised in devout Catholic families and accepted the Church's positions on sexuality without question. The hypocrisy of the Church hierarchy regarding such matters had not yet come to the fore.

They were also the product of their times. In addition, their discovery of Rita as lesbian came on the heels of the revelation that our brother, Ed, was gay. At one point, they pleaded with Reet to start dating boys. She agreed. After graduating from high school on Long Island, Reet moved to Reading to attend the radiologic technology program at Reading Hospital. We met several guys she dated and occasionally had them over for dinner. One of her boyfriends was a nice guy named Steve. During one of our parents' visits from Florida, all of us went out to dinner together so they could meet him. Not much later, Rita, Steve, JoAnne, and I traveled to New York for an overnight visit to attend the wedding of one of our cousins. That Sunday over dinner, Reet told us that dating Steve had been a sham. Steve was gay! He was an acquaintance who agreed to date Reet just to mollify our parents.

Reet told us that, even while dating guys, she knew she was not being true to herself. During a visit by Rita and Ann to my mom in Florida, it came to a head. Under the impression that Rita had resolved her "sexuality issue," my mom inadvertently witnessed a subtle display of affection between Rita and Ann. She knew then that Rita's experiment with dating guys had come to an end. She responded by saying, "I should have stopped having children after Bobby!"

Until that Sunday dinner with Rita and Melissa, I knew none of this. The idea that my mom would have essentially told Rita that she wished she had never been born was shocking. I couldn't imagine it. Rita said that she simply replied, "You're gonna lose me, Mom. This is who I am."

From that point on, my mom must have swallowed hard, prayed a lot, and known that if she wanted to keep Rita in her life, she had no choice. For her part, Rita remained a loving daughter. She and Ann, who my mom grew to love as a second daughter, made annual trips to Florida, which continued after our mom met and married Jim. However, a deep cut always leaves a scar, and I believe Rita carried the pain of that cut for the rest of her life. Reflecting on my mom's cruel comment, I have come to see Rita's reply in the context of the quote attributed to Jesus in the crucifixion account in the Gospel of Luke: "Father, forgive them, for they know not what they do." Or what they say.

By not responding in kind to a deeply hurtful statement that must have rocked her to the core, Rita offered my mom the opportunity to sustain their relationship, but it would have to be a relationship based on respect and acceptance. I also came to realize that this incident shed light on Reet's devastation when Hershey Medical Center told her that they would not accept her as my kidney donor. Rita was incapable of manipulative or vindictive notions, but I believe that the gift of her kidney to me was her ultimate answer to our mom's cruel comment.

Our heads were spinning as we drove home that night. We felt conflicted that Rita had ended her previous relationship. Ann had become our close friend, and we regarded her as part of our family. We resolved to continue that friendship. But my primary feeling was one of relief that a family secret was now out in the open. Perhaps for the first time in her life, Rita could be confident that she was unconditionally loved and accepted by all of us. Her sexuality made no difference to anyone. Most importantly, she seemed truly happy.

A few weeks later, Rita and Melissa accompanied JoAnne and me to Philadelphia for the ceremony at which I would receive my doctorate from the Pennsylvania College of Optometry School of Audiology. From my standpoint, it was great to see my little sister display affection for the woman she loved and receive affection in return. Afterward, we dined at an Italian restaurant in celebration of my doctorate and Reet and Melissa as a couple. During dinner, chatting and sated from our meal, Rita offhandedly mentioned that she had been noticing some abdominal bloating and cramping lately. What woman hasn't? None of us had any inkling that it was anything serious.

## CHAPTER THIRTEEN

## *Good Summer*

As happens every few years, the Christian celebration of Pentecost coincided with Memorial Day weekend in 2004. We saw Melissa at Mass that morning, but Rita hadn't accompanied her. She told us that Reet hadn't been feeling well, the abdominal discomfort she had mentioned the week before had persisted and even worsened somewhat, and she was running a slight fever. At some point during the week, she had checked with her doctor, who thought she had the flu.

JoAnne and I spent Monday, Memorial Day, with college friends who were visiting their daughter and son-in-law in Carlisle, PA. When we returned home that evening, there was a frantic message from Melissa on our answering machine. She and Rita were at the Reading Hospital Emergency Room. Rita's pain had worsened to the extent that dealing with it couldn't be put off any longer. On top of that, the doctors were talking about cancer.

It had been exactly twenty years earlier that I had received the Memorial Day phone call from my mom in Florida, telling me that our dad had died suddenly. Then, on Memorial Day twelve years later, Rita's apartment was damaged by a large fire that broke out in a nearby warehouse in Reading. She was visiting our mom at the time, so it was my turn to make a wrenching Memorial Day phone call, this time to tell Rita that her apartment building was in flames. Now, once again, our family was visited with another devastating Memorial Day call.

We wasted no time driving to the Reading Hospital ER, where we found Melissa reeling with the possibility that Rita was dealing with an advanced stage of ovarian cancer. A referral to a gynecological oncologist was in the works. For now, the plan was to admit her so the fluid that had built up in her pelvic area could be drained and assessed for the presence of cancer cells.

Melissa led us to Rita's bed in the emergency accommodations area, where we found my sister distraught and red-eyed. We embraced in a teary hug for what seemed like an eternity. The scene seemed surreal. Just a few short weeks earlier, we had been looking forward to this new chapter in all our lives. Now, in the blink of an eye, it seemed that chapter might be tragically cut short. When she could finally speak, her first comment seared into me.

"I finally found the person I want to spend the rest of my life with . . ." She didn't have to say any more.

Words were difficult. I searched for some source of comfort and sensed that all of us, especially Rita, needed something to look forward to: a goal that would enable us to look beyond this potentially devastating moment. It had to be something that meant a lot to her. I didn't have to ponder it long: Ireland.

I sat on the edge of her bed, put my hands on her shoulders, and looked her resolutely in the eyes. We would return to Ireland, where she could show Melissa the country whose culture, landscape, history, and people had taken up residence in our hearts.

"We're going to get back to Ireland, Reet. You and Melissa, JoAnne and I. When this is over, we're going to go back to Ireland."

Through her tears, she nodded. "Yes, yes, we will."

In truth, at this point, none of us seemed quite sure of anything, let alone transatlantic travel, but at least a goal had been set. We had visited Ireland twice before: in 1995, prior to the World Transplant Games in Manchester, England, and again in 1998. We often spoke of returning. When Rita needed to look beyond whatever would soon transpire, she could look forward to returning to Ireland—this time with Melissa, the woman she loved.

Rita was discharged from the hospital a few days later and scheduled for surgery the following Monday. The Saturday before surgery, JoAnne helped Melissa arrange a prayer service at their home and invited our pastor, Father Dave Devlin, to preside. Many of our friends and theirs came, including Ann. Father Dave blessed Rita as all of us held her up in prayer. She seemed in good spirits, which were buoyed by the outpouring of love and concern evident that morning. She was beginning to draw on a renewed sense of determination and strength to face her upcoming surgery and whatever lay beyond.

Throughout that time, as we grappled with this bleak turn of events and its implications, I found myself recalling one of our songs at Mass that Pentecost Sunday. One verse in particular became my prayer: "Send us good summer, O Lord. Winters have chilled us and stilled us too long."[9] Yes, send us good summer—send us some light into this dark space.

On Monday, the surgeon removed a large pelvic mass and Rita's ovaries and uterus. He came down from the OR to talk to Melissa, JoAnne, and I and said Reet came through the procedure well but declined to speculate exactly what type of tumor he had encountered until he received confirmation from pathology. Within a day, he reported to Melissa and Rita that she was, in fact, dealing with ovarian cancer, Stage 3C. Simplified, this meant that the substantial tumor mass had not spread to other organs, such as the lungs or liver, although tumor cells were found in the fluid that had accumulated in her pleural (around the lungs) spaces. That her cancer was not Stage 4 offered a modicum of comfort. She would be discharged in a few days and, after healing for a month, would begin chemotherapy.

The day-to-day burden of attending to Rita's needs, taking her to appointments, and, most important, providing emotional support would

---

9   Text by Dan Schutte, copyright 1985, OCP. All rights reserved. Used with permission.

fall on Melissa. In turn, JoAnne and I resolved to be as supportive of each of them as we could. I occasionally found myself glancing at Melissa and wondering just how this young woman had arrived in our lives at this time. JoAnne and I could not have offered the kind of comfort and intimacy Rita would need to draw on for strength on a day-to-day basis. Melissa was unflinching in her commitment to my sister. I was beginning to see that the angels that appear at the exact places and times they're most needed aren't necessarily the kind with wings!

About a month after discharge, Rita began chemotherapy. At that time, the standard chemo for ovarian cancer was a two-drug regimen. However, Reading Hospital was participating in a national trial that featured a three-drug protocol, also referred to as a "triple." She elected to participate in the trial after being advised that outcomes thus far suggested that it was at least as effective as the standard approach and may well offer more benefit. Hair loss was a certainty, as well as fatigue and dangerously low blood counts that might result in deviation from the protocol's schedule, which called for chemo infusions every three weeks. It was possible that she would be dropped from the study if the schedule could not be maintained, and she would be transferred to the standard two-drug regimen.

As if to defy cancer and the side effects of treatment, Rita asked Melissa to shave off her hair once it started to fall out in clumps. One of the doctors I worked with knew of Rita's condition and suggested that I have my head shaved. At first, I casually brushed off the idea, but I gradually realized that it would be a wonderful way to show solidarity and offer some emotional support. JoAnne was one-hundred-percent on board. About a week after Rita started chemo and just as her hair was beginning to rapidly disappear, mine vanished under the barber's clippers. I was glad it was summer. As fall approached, I found out that bare heads can be very cold.

The evening of my shearing, Ann invited Rita, Melissa, JoAnne, and I over for dessert. Despite their split, Ann and Reet had remained friends. I wore a baseball cap into the house, but Rita could tell as soon as she saw me that something was different. As I took off my cap, I told her that my hair had begun to fall out a few days before, and by that morning it was all gone. With as much gravity as I could muster, I lied that I had consulted my nephrologist, who told me that there were case reports of transplant recipients "shadowing" physical changes in their living donors. Just to be sure, they wanted me to have a head biopsy.

She looked at me with bemusement, shook her head, and replied, "You *need* a head biopsy!"

She was probably right. I think she appreciated the gesture, and we all had a good laugh.

Even though she eventually had to be removed from the three-drug protocol because of toxicities, which included sustained low blood counts and extreme fatigue, chemo was effective in substantially lowering Reet's Ca125, an ovarian cancer marker measured by blood tests. In the fall, she and Melissa flew down to Wilmington, NC, for a long weekend, where we joined them and our other NC family members. On a warm, sunny afternoon, all of us took a ferry to the picturesque harbor town of Southport, where we toured the town on bikes and stopped to enjoy lunch at a dockside seafood restaurant. Relaxing over beer and seafood sandwiches as the waves lapped gently against the pilings, I allowed the possibility that the good summer I had prayed for had arrived, albeit a bit late. As 2004 yielded to 2005, it began to look like there was light at the end of the tunnel, from which Reet could anticipate emerging. Her hair made a thick and surprisingly curly comeback, she regained some energy, and she had returned to work.

In July all of us traveled to Wilmington for the wedding of Dave and his fiancé, Teresa. Reet and Melissa danced and carried on for hours at the festive reception. A few weeks later, Amy joined the two of them for a long weekend visit to the Finger Lakes region of Upstate New York, Melissa's old stomping grounds as a graduate of Ithaca College. Reet's periodic checkups showed no evidence of cancer on physical examination and a sustained low Ca125. We were beginning to entertain the hope that Rita would be one of the few who would be blessed with long-term survival of a disease that, diagnosed in its advanced stages, was viewed as a killer. As the holidays approached, it looked as though all of us had a lot to be thankful for. The year 2005 had indeed been a good year.

Then, in early 2006, her Ca125 began to creep up, suggesting that her cancer had returned.

Over dinner at a Mexican restaurant one evening, JoAnne asked Rita, "How concerned are you?"

She replied, "I'm terrified."

A physical exam soon revealed a small nodule that had developed in her lower pelvic area, and a subsequent biopsy confirmed a recurrence. She was advised that if there was one lesion, there likely were more. Instead of surgery, a recommendation was made for another round of chemo. Despite this setback, Rita and Melissa continued with plans to fly to Mexico City to visit Amy, who had taken up residence there a few years before. They would fly from Philadelphia to Charlotte, where they would meet up with Dave and Teresa, who would be flying in from Wilmington. The four of them would then fly on to Mexico.

It turned out to be a great visit. Amy showed them some of the unique sights and sounds of that vibrant, energetic metropolis, as well as some of her own haunts, including a bar that featured pulque, a Mexican "cocktail" of cactus and tequila and a restroom that offered phone-book pages as toilet paper. One of the more memorable events revolved around an attempt to speak Spanish while placing an order for a dish featuring rice, various quesos (cheese), and, of course, beans. They turned out to be placing an order for male gonads.

Their trip included a visit to Teotihuacan, the well-preserved ruins of an early first-millennium city that had been occupied by an Indigenous Mesoamerican culture. On the one-hour bus ride, Rita fell asleep but suddenly popped up when she heard Madonna's song "Hung Up" over the bus stereo and went into some of the associated dance gyrations, at least those that could be performed while seated on a moving vehicle.

Teotihuacan features temples and pyramids that honored whatever gods and goddesses were in vogue at the time. Visitors blessed with some degree of fitness and a sense of adventure often attempt to climb them, no small feat since they are situated over a mile above sea level. Reet decided not to let a little chemotherapy, associated anemia, and ovarian cancer stop her. Under the watchful eyes of Melissa and the others, she climbed to the top of one of the temples, as if to show the world, including herself, that her indomitable spirit would not be easily conquered. Bus ride included, the day at Teotihuacan turned out to be the highlight of the trip.

By late spring, Rita had completed her second round of chemo, which, like the first, succeeded in reducing her Ca125 to acceptable levels, and she was in remission once again. It was time to make plans for the trip to Ireland that I had promised two years earlier in the Reading Hospital ER.

Our mother was born in Ireland in 1925 and immigrated with her parents when she was three. She and my grandparents viewed their homeland as the world they left behind with little desire to return. Yet, like most sons and daughters of immigrants, we harbored a curiosity about our ancestral homeland. As soon as we heard that the 1995 World Transplant Games would be held in Manchester, England, it was a foregone conclusion that we would first visit Ireland while we were "in the neighborhood." While Dave's summer employment precluded taking two full weeks off to travel (he would meet up with us in Manchester), Amy, Rita, JoAnne, and I landed at Shannon Airport in the west of Ireland on a Sunday in early August. We carried with us copies of my grandparents' marriage certificate from St. Michael's Roman Catholic Church in Cootehill, County Cavan, as well as my mother's baptism certificate from Sacred Heart Church in Clones (Klo'-niss) County Monaghan.

On the morning of one particularly magical day, we spoke to people in Cootehill who had known my grandmother's family. Then we ventured to Clones, where Church baptism records led us to the country home where my mother was born. Later, we met a man who knew my grandfather some seventy years before. He pointed out the home where our grandparents had lived and where my mom's four older siblings were born. Rita and I stood on the sidewalk in front of the modest row home a stone's throw from the center of town as JoAnne took a picture from across the street. At that moment, I heard a window slide open, and the woman of the house invited us in for a quick tour.

As we drove to our B and B that evening, I couldn't help but wonder, *Is this a dream? Did all of that really happen?* Perhaps we had all been marionettes on invisible strings deftly guided by my grandparents who were looking down on us with appreciation that we had cared enough to seek out our Irish roots. Until then, I had always known of my Irish ancestry, but it had not meant a whole lot. In addition, JoAnne's maternal ancestry hailed from County Cork. Now Ireland had come alive for all of us.

Three years later, Rita joined JoAnne and me on a ten-day adventure in the rugged west and southwest of Ireland, highlighted by a day on Inishmore, one of the Aran Islands. We developed an affinity for that beautiful country, its people, and its music. After those trips, Reet would come over to our house and play the piano or guitar to accompany some Irish folk song sessions. A few years later, we began a St. Patrick's Day tradition of turning our home into an Irish pub where Rita and our friends would gather for a meal and a pint, followed by a ceilidh (Irish songfest). We had embraced our heritage and spoke of returning to Ireland again. We never could have imagined the circumstances under which that would happen.

Prior to the trip, Rita and Melissa arranged to hold a commitment ceremony. It would be a public statement of their love for each other in the presence of friends and family. I had never heard of a commitment ceremony, but I reasoned that heterosexual couples enjoy such affirmation via their weddings and receptions. I recalled a Catholic wedding from years before when the celebrant priest shocked everyone in attendance by announcing that he would *not* be marrying the happy couple that day—they would be marrying each other! In that context, a commitment ceremony made perfect liturgical sense. The acceptance of same-sex marriage was almost a decade away and even now has not penetrated some of our more ossified Christian theologies.

On the afternoon of Sunday, August 5, about fifty of us, including Melissa's dad and step mom and my mom and Jim, gathered in the flowery yard of Melissa's business partner who offered the location for the occasion. Some friends from our church, Bill and Michele Cambardella and Johanna Kelly and Dan Buckley and their kids, were part of our celebration. They knew Rita well and were glad to join us. Bill and Johanna lent their considerable musical talents. It was lost on none of us that this celebration of love could not be held in the Catholic Church in which we gathered every Sunday to share our faith, despite the fact that our many friends in the congregation knew of and were supportive of Reet and Melissa as a couple, and our Pastor, Father Dave Devlin, had been present to all of us during Rita's illness and treatment. The institutional Roman Catholic Church and the Body of Christ in the pews are often two very different entities.

I had been asked to provide a welcome for everyone. I knew exactly what I would say. My words reflected my thoughts that went back to that plaintive prayer two years before when we were confronted with Reet's bleak diagnosis. I had prayed for "good summer." Now here we were, Rita and Melissa's family and friends gathered on a sunny summer afternoon in celebration of their relationship. For the moment at least, our prayers had been answered. Friends read moving, often humorous tributes. Then Rita and Melissa exchanged written vows in which they pledged their love and commitment to each other. It was a heartfelt affirmation of two women joined as one. After we enjoyed some delicious food and drink, my mother and Jim contributed by leading everyone in a lively line-dancing session on the spacious deck as evening fell. It had been two years since I learned of my mom's harsh words those many years before that had wounded Rita so deeply. Yet, there was my mom, celebrating the union of her daughter and another woman. I wanted so much to hold on to the moment, but the gnawing possibility was always present; how many more good summers would we have?

That sobering thought was soon to be realized. In late August, Reet's Ca125 blood test came back elevated once again. With our long-anticipated trip to Ireland set to begin within a week, her cancer was most likely back. The doctors gave her a choice: Begin another round of chemo immediately or go to Ireland and start treatment when she returned. Implied was the suggestion that she might best take this trip now because, in the not-too-distant future, her illness was likely to progress to the point at which such an undertaking would be impossible. Her decision came quickly. We would go to Ireland.

Dave, Teresa, Melissa, Rita, and Amy at Chapultepec Park, Mexico City, March 2006

Melissa and Rita at their commitment ceremony, August 5, 2006

CHAPTER FOURTEEN

## *Ireland*

JoAnne and I made plans to get together with Reet and Melissa at their house shortly before our departure to finalize our itinerary. I was the last one to arrive. It was the first time I had seen Rita since the news of her latest recurrence. As she opened the door to let me in, we shared a silent hug that lingered a little longer than it might have under different circumstances. Then she pointed over to Melissa and JoAnne, who were kneeling on the living room floor, pondering a large map of Ireland.

"Let's not waste any time," she said as she led me over to join them.

Her stark prophecy resonated . . . *Let's not waste any time.*

On the morning of September 2, 2006, we landed in Belfast after a six-and-a-half-hour flight. Blue skies had greeted us on our previous visits to Ireland, but this time we were pelted with rain as we found our rental car and drove to our B and B just outside of Belfast. Our plan was to unpack and take a short rest before exploring that historically violence-wracked city. By the time we settled in, Rita was extremely tired and in pain. The flight had taken a lot out of her in her already weakened condition. She decided to stay behind and rest for the afternoon while Melissa, JoAnne, and I checked out the city. The trip we had anticipated for so long wasn't getting off to a good start.

As we found our way around bustling Belfast, the three of us silently pondered whether this trip had been a wise decision. At dinner that evening, Reet barely ate a thing. It was clear that, stoic as she was, she was in pain and couldn't wait to get back to the B and B. Rather than a joyous, spirited return to our ancestral home, the trip we had talked about for over two years was proving to be a wrenching confirmation of just how sick Rita was. That night JoAnne and I began a bedtime prayer that turned into a sobbing embrace. We had no idea how all of us would manage to get through the next ten days. We even entertained the possibility of an early flight home.

At breakfast the following morning, Reet was noticeably better, in less pain, and not as fatigued. The sky had brightened, allowing us to look forward to a Sunday drive along the Antrim Coast toward our next destination. We were given directions to a picturesque country church in a pleasant setting, arrived a "wee bit" late, and found seats in the choir loft. As we participated in and took comfort from the familiar prayers and rituals, I began to allow that perhaps our Irish adventure hadn't been a mistake after all. Hopefully, Rita's improved condition would hold up and she could share Ireland's magic with Melissa.

We found our next B and B just outside of the town of Cushendun on the northeast coast of County Antrim, checked in for two nights, and headed to our destination for the day, the Carrick-a-Rede Bridge, a rickety span of rope and wooden planking, suspended a hundred feet above the churning water, between the rocky coast and a small island about seventy feet offshore. On the way, we stopped at a scenic overlook, where impossibly green fields, crisscrossed by low stone walls, yielded to cliffs descending abruptly to the sea. We had experienced this kind of breathtaking scenery on our previous trips. Now the quintessential rugged Irish coastline was laid out before us once again.

We got out of the car, breathed in the crisp sea air, and stood in awe of the jewel of creation before us. I looked over at Rita. She wore a smile of satisfaction.

"This is why we came, Bobby," she reflected quietly. "This is why we came."

My eyes moistened, though I knew they'd better dry out quickly because I had a lot of precise driving to do along narrow, curvy, coastal roads perched above the steep cliffs of Ireland's northeast coast. Shortly thereafter, the first of several rainbows we would encounter that day made its appearance. I doubt that even Noah himself appreciated that message of hope as much as we did.

Over the next few days, we made our way across Antrim's north coast on our way to Donegal in Ireland's northwest. We visited Giant's Causeway, a unique geologic formation that had formed ages ago as the result of a coastal volcanic eruption. The hot lava flowing into the frigid ocean water had immediately crystallized into 30,000 hexagonal basalt columns that formed stepping stones along the cliffside. The four of us made our way down the trail, toward the shoreline, and came across a snail making its slow, lonely way across our path.

Rita exclaimed, "It's a shellicky bookey," (shall-uh-key-BOO-key) the name given to snails by children growing up in rural Ireland a few generations ago. Years earlier, our whole family had learned the "Shellicky bookey Song" from an album of Irish folk music. The four of us broke out in a spirited but disharmonic rendition of the Shellicky bookey Song. At the time, I could not have known how our shellicky bookey moment would come back to me in a way I never could have foreseen.

Later that day, we stopped to see the ruins of Dunluce Castle. Built in the thirteenth century by the earl of Ulster, Dunluce juts out dramatically on a narrow spit of land. In 1588 a galleon of the Spanish Armada crashed on the rocks nearby, one of many such calamities that befell that formidable fleet along the coasts of Ireland and Scotland, as it was harassed by violent storms and English privateers. We wandered through its myriad chambers, imagining life in a medieval castle with enemies lurking both landward and seaward.

In a room that had been the earl's bedchamber, our curiosity was piqued by what appeared to be a very low opening at floor level, extending up about two feet, clearly an unusual place for a window. A guide explained that, no, this wasn't a window but simply an outlet through which the earl could relieve himself. Rita pondered the implications momentarily, then quipped, "Men were always so lucky. All they had to do was aim Mr. Winky . . ." as if to bemoan another example of the unequal playing field encountered by women over time immemorial.

Thus edified, we began to make our way back to the car, until I motioned for us to stop and ponder for a moment Reet's profound historical and cultural insight.

I looked at her and, with great deliberation, queried, "Mr. Winky? Since when does an anatomically knowledgeable X-ray tech refer to a certain component of male anatomy as Mr. Winky?"

She assured me that she rarely employed the term in a clinical environment. Intellectually sated, we got into the car and continued our journey. It would not be Mr. Winky's last appearance, figuratively speaking.

Once in County Donegal, we checked in at our B and B in the town of Buncrana. It was dreary and rainy as we settled in for dinner at the Drift Inn, a pub/restaurant located a stone's throw from cold Lough Swilly. The inn's dark interior, warmed by roaring fireplaces, told us that we had made the right choice, an observation that was confirmed when Fionna, our cute, petite server with a brogue as thick as Irish stew, brought our selections, including my steamed garlic mussels perched on the edge of a deep bowl of light cream garlic sauce. Competing with the mussels for my attention and a share of the sauce were thick slices of crusty Irish brown bread. The established ritual was to scoop out the contents of a mussel with a shellfish fork, dip it into the garlic sauce, follow that up with hunks of bread, then wash it all down with copious swigs of Guinness. It was the best meal I had had on any of our trips to Ireland and one of the best meals of my life. Along with the Guinness, the conversation flowed easily, often punctuated by references to Mr. Winky and gales of raucous laughter. Rita and Melissa were thoroughly having fun after several interesting and enjoyable days in Ireland's north. In the warm glow of a Donegal pub, our chilling reality was put at bay at least for an evening.

From Donegal, we made our way along the northwest coast and settled into a B and B in County Sligo, near Clew Bay a few miles outside of Westport. There, we explored some offshore islands and learned that, more than four centuries earlier, the waters of Clew Bay were plied by one Grace O'Malley. Unlike many Irish legends, this one appears to have a historical basis. As a child, young Grace sailed with her father, who commanded a fleet of privateers. When Grace grew up and married, her husband eventually came to command the fleet, not by virtue of any particular skills in navigation or piracy but via the inheritance laws at the time. After he managed to get himself killed in a local interclan squabble, Grace's second husband, equally incompetent, inherited the fleet. When he met the same fate, the 200 or so (presumably male) pirates asked Grace to take command because of the skills in navigation and piracy she had learned at her father's side.

Thus, the fact/legend of the Pirate Queen, new to us until our time in County Sligo, became part of Irish lore. Many months later, when JoAnne and I took possession of a tawny-red terrier-mix rescue dog, Grace O'Malley seemed a perfect name that would both reflect an independent spirit and serve as a living reminder of Grace O'Malley, Rita, and our last days in Ireland.

We were looking forward to the pub scene for "trad" music and found Hoban's in Westport, where JoAnne and I spent two evenings in the back room of this establishment largely frequented by locals. The music was lively and fun, and the evenings passed quickly. Trad sessions don't usually get under way until 9:30 at night and often continue well into the wee hours. Rita loved music, especially Irish music, but, by this time in our journey, she was experiencing more fatigue and pain and chose to rest and retire early. Melissa stayed by her side despite JoAnne's offer for one of us to stay with Reet so Melissa could enjoy an evening at an Irish pub. That is pretty much how the whole trip went—Melissa, ever watchful and supportive. It was obvious that the vows she and Rita exchanged on that bright summer afternoon barely a month earlier had been heartfelt and real.

Not far from our B and B, Croagh Patrick (St. Patrick's Mountain) loomed over Clew Bay and beckoned adventurous hikers. Depending on the weather, its peak could yield spectacular views of the Bay to the north and hauntingly beautiful Connemara to the south. It could also be shrouded in clouds and mist. Irish legend holds that, in the fourth century, St. Patrick himself ascended its rocky slopes and, upon arriving at the summit, fasted forty days and forty nights before descending and proceeding to bring Christianity to Ireland. Unlike the Grace O'Malley story, this one is a Christian-era extension of an Irish mythology that dates back thousands of years.

The idea of a pilgrimage to a religious site, with its inexplicable link to a sense of the presence of the Almighty, is an inherent part of Irish Catholic spirituality. The tradition of climbing Croagh Patrick held that prayers for healing and other intentions could be offered at the top. JoAnne and I felt compelled to climb Croagh Patrick for several reasons. Both of us grew up in strong Irish Catholic traditions and wanted to honor our ancestors who had left this beautiful but troubled land with little more than their Catholic faith. In addition, we were also aware that, in another time, Rita would have climbed Croagh Patrick with us. JoAnne and I ascended St. Patrick's Mountain for her and, in many ways, with her. If Rita couldn't join us, at least her kidney would.

Those were our thoughts, some spoken, some silent, as we reached the peak, which, on this day, was enshrouded in clouds. We found the small mountaintop chapel closed but nevertheless offered prayers, some in gratitude for a safe journey thus far, others for healing for Reet and strength and peace for all of us.

On the way down, the clouds began to lift, and we were treated to spectacular views of the land and sea around us. Croagh Patrick marked the beginning of our last full day in Ireland. We had started early and arrived back at our B and B a little before noon to rejoin Rita and Melissa. After checking out, we headed for our final B and B just outside of Ennis in beautiful County Clare, where our first journey to Ireland had begun eleven years before. Our Irish adventure had yielded memorable moments, laughter, and tears. It had been the third trip to that magical land for Rita, JoAnne, and me. Unsaid—but very much weighing on all of us as we took off from Shannon Airport and caught wistful glimpses of the verdant landscape as it gave way to the rocky cliffs of Ireland's west coast—was that it would likely be Rita's last.

The Antrim Coast

Me, JoAnne, Rita, and Melissa at Giants Causeway after encountering the shellicky bookie. "At the time, I had no way of knowing that our shellicky bookey moment would come back to me in a way I never could have foreseen."

Dunluce Castle

"Men were always so lucky. All they had to do was aim Mr. Winky."

Fionna, our waitress, Melissa, JoAnne, Rita, and the ruins of my steamed garlic mussels at the Drift Inn, Buncrana, County Donegal

The Croagh Patrick welcoming committee

CHAPTER FIFTEEN

## *My Body Is Torn*

Rita's health stabilized for the 2006 holidays, a Christmas gift for all of us. Her Ca125 continued to be elevated but had not risen significantly, and her pelvic exams failed to reveal anything remarkable. However, by early spring, her condition had begun to deteriorate, marked by a few brief hospitalizations for one complication after another. In addition, chemo treatments continued to take their toll. To help mitigate some of the severe side effects, they were accompanied by IV steroids that gave her a rosy glow, which belied her true condition.

For several years, she and Melissa had participated in our church choir, Melissa as a vocalist and Rita on guitar. Now, as the Easter Triduum (Holy Thursday, Good Friday, Saturday Easter Vigil) approached, Reet hadn't felt well enough to participate in rehearsals and was absent for Thursday Mass. We were surprised and happy, then, to see her walk into church for the Good Friday service. Rather than standing to play guitar, she joined us in the choir. However, that encouraging event was juxtaposed against a grim new reality. In the couple of weeks since JoAnne and I had last seen her, the rosy glow had been replaced by the first signs of the drawn, gray pallor of the terminal cancer patient who had begun to lose the final battle. Until then, we had held on to small threads of denial. *Maybe she can keep up the good fight for a long time, even confound the odds and beat this.* When I saw her face that evening as she approached the choir seats, those threads were cut once and for all.

As is the tradition, our Good Friday service began in silence. Then, following the first of three scripture readings, the choir sang the responsorial refrain, "Father, be my refuge, into your hands I commend my spirit,"[10] and led the congregation in repeating it. Then we sang the first verse, led the congregation in the refrain again, and began the second verse. Over my own voice, I could hear the plaintive cry of the sopranos: "My eyes now burn with the salt of my tears; my soul has been broken; my body is torn."[11] They were the last words I could sing.

In every Catholic Church, the figure of the crucified Jesus is the visual focal point, as well as the emotional heart of the liturgy, never more so than on Good Friday. Before us is displayed the unlikely, no-strings-attached offer of suffering yielding redemption and wholeness, affirming our flawed humanity as the object of the self-emptying love of the Creator. I looked at Rita, then up at the crucifix. My eyes saw the image of the crucified Jesus, but my heart and soul saw my sister: my terminally ill, lesbian little sister whose sacrifice had given me life. The seminal Christian message of selfless love had become, for me, visceral and intensely personal.

After the dismissal, I gave Reet a hug as she received everyone's warm greetings. I have many times pondered the moment when I saw our humanity nailed to that cross in the form of my sister, her body torn, her soul very much unbroken.

Despite her condition, she and Melissa made plans to visit Amy in Mexico City shortly after Easter. JoAnne and I thought it was unwise, to say the least, but it was not our place to question. They had discussed it for quite some time, and abandoning their venture would amount to surrendering to Rita's cancer. She was much sicker now than she had

---

10   "Be My Refuge." Text copyright 2001, Daniel L. Schutte. Published by OCP. All rights reserved. Used with permission.
11   "Be My Refuge." Text copyright 2001, Daniel L. Schutte. Published by OCP. All rights reserved. Used with permission.

been at the time of our Ireland trip, a journey that, while it ended well and gave us some special moments, was stressful and scary for all of us, especially Melissa. Nonetheless, Rita was determined to make one last trip to Mexico to see Amy.

We asked if we could help in any way. I offered to drive them to the airport. It would mean picking them up on Sunday at 4 a.m. With heartfelt appreciation, Reet initially declined my offer.

"You don't need to do that!" she said. We held each other's gaze for a long moment in which words seemed inadequate.

"Reet . . ." I managed. I held out my arms. She understood.

*Reet, I owe you my life and well-being. I owe you everything. Maybe I don't* have *to do this, but I* need *to do this.*

I pulled into their driveway at 4 a.m. as planned, helped Melissa get their luggage into the trunk, and waited for Rita to come out. She walked to the car, carrying an emesis basin, which had become her constant companion, not exactly a good omen with which to begin a taxing trip to Mexico. She looked awful. An elderly neighbor had asked Reet to drive her around on some errands the day before. She had planned to spend the day resting up for the trip but didn't have the heart to say no. It took a lot out of her, and it showed—another ominous start to an international trip.

An hour and fifteen minutes later, we arrived at the departure terminal of Philadelphia International Airport. As I removed their luggage from the trunk, Melissa went to get a wheelchair, and Rita waited in the car. Five minutes later, Melissa emerged. Rita got out, thanked me, and dismissively flipped the emesis basin back into the car as if in defiance of the cancer ravaging her body. She sat down in the wheelchair, and the two of them headed into the terminal and off to Mexico.

I watched as long as I could until the crowd swallowed them up. I had grown accustomed to seeing my gutsy little sister look adversity straight in the eye, but this was above and beyond. I prayed as I drove home from the airport. Reet, Melissa, and Amy would need all the help they could get over the next few days.

That evening, we received a tearful call from Amy. It was the first time she had seen "the look" we had seen on Good Friday. We had tried to prepare her, but she was shocked anyway. That phone call was, for JoAnne and me, a long-distance replay of our sobbing embrace in Ireland eight months earlier. Amy was devastated and could not fathom what the next few days would bring.

It was, of necessity, a low-key visit. Once again, as in Ireland, Melissa was by Rita's side every step of the way. They attempted an outing to Coyoacán, a charming neighborhood south of the city, but had to abandon midcourse because of Rita's pain and fatigue. This time, there were no triumphant visits to pyramids, nor tales of hilarious restaurant antics. They returned home as scheduled a few days later. Once again, adversity had blinked. But all of us knew it was only a matter of time until it would ultimately win out.

## CHAPTER SIXTEEN

## *In the Arms of the Angel*

Amy flew home from Mexico City for her birthday, June 9 . . . but primarily to see Rita. Her timing was good. Reet had been admitted to the hospital once again. Her disease had progressed to the point at which her gastric motility had become severely restricted. It had become difficult to ingest nourishment and eliminate waste, and she was experiencing increased pain.

Dave and Teresa had driven up from North Carolina. All of us, including Melissa, who somehow seemed omnipresent, celebrated Amy's birthday in Reet's hospital room. We even managed to smuggle in some beer. The nursing staff didn't make an issue of it and even seemed a little envious.

At one point, Rita announced that she had to use the toilet and made her way slowly into the bathroom. As she exited, a nurse asked her how productive her toilet session had been.

With mock pride, she announced, "Two little turds!"

It seemed important to recognize and celebrate even the most absurd of any positive signs that had become few and far between. I raised my beer and proposed to all present, "To the turds," to which everyone replied enthusiastically.

With a bemused smile, the nurse acknowledged that she had never heard anyone raise a glass to turds before. Reference to our bizarre toast most likely never ended up in her nurse's notes.

It wasn't the only time the nursing staff looked the other way. At Rita's request, Melissa brought Clancy, their small, gray fur-ball dog, for a visit. The same nurse came into the room and noticed Clancy resting comfortably on the sheets, covering Rita's abdomen. Reet, for her part, didn't miss an opportunity for a wisecrack.

Pointing to Clancy, she quipped, "Nurse, there's a gray furry growth protruding from my abdomen."

No doubt, that didn't make the nurse's notes either.

The next day, to improve Rita's ability to take in nourishment, the doctors attempted to insert a nasogastric (feeding) tube. Despite having a famously high pain threshold, Reet couldn't tolerate it. Her gastric system's motility had become so restricted by the cancer filling her pelvis and abdomen that it simply was not compliant enough to allow the tube to be located comfortably. They withdrew it almost immediately.

Not long after, I received a distressed call from Melissa. The doctors had come into the room for a conference with her and Rita. They could no longer justify continued treatment for Rita's cancer. Her choice would be to stay in the hospital and spend her remaining days there or go home on hospice.

I left my office and hurried over to Reet's room. To say that she and Melissa were distraught is an understatement. Though this moment had seemed inevitable for months, if not longer, they looked dazed, almost shocked. I sat on the edge of Rita's bed. We hugged each other and cried. After what seemed like an eternity, she broke the embrace, looked straight at me, and once again tried to muster the defiance that had characterized this and past health battles.

"I'm not giving up," she said with as much conviction as she could offer.

I nodded in affirmation but could say no more. It had been a little over three years to the day that we had played out a similar scene in the emergency room accommodations area. This time, there would be no Ireland trip; there would be no "good summer."

Amy had just returned to Mexico City a few days before the doctor's decision. We called her, and, without hesitation, she said that she would fly home as soon as she could. Within an hour, she secured permission to leave her position as a sixth-grade teacher at an American private school and flew home the next day. My mom and Jim drove up from Florida, making the trip they had made many times before but under far different circumstances.

After Rita's discharge and return home, Melissa, amid her devastation, coordinated hospice services, which would include a hospital bed, nurse's visits, and pain management. And so, our dreaded vigil began. JoAnne, my mom, and Amy managed to hold down the fort at Rita and Melissa's home during the day, allowing Melissa to continue to work full-time. Amy, in particular, would spend most of the day with Rita.

On the last weekend in June, my stepsister came down from New Hampshire, and Dave and Teresa drove up from Wilmington. Everyone acknowledged that they were there to offer an unstated goodbye. Teresa, by that time, was not quite seven months along in her first pregnancy, and it showed. On Saturday evening, all of us got together on the deck of our home. We carried out a comfortable recliner for Reet.

As I was grilling sausages, I noticed that Teresa had pulled up a chair and was sitting next to her. At one point, Rita reached over and placed her hand on Teresa's abdomen to feel the movement of the child she must have known she would never see. The poignancy of the moment was almost too much to bear. I found some solace in the fact that my eyes were already moist from grill smoke.

On Monday, July 2, Reet became noticeably confused. By Tuesday, it had become bad enough that Amy called Melissa and asked her to come home from work ASAP. During evening office hours, I received a call from JoAnne telling me to go to Rita and Melissa's, where she, my mom, Jim, and Amy had gathered. Rita's condition was deteriorating rapidly. Before leaving work, I walked into the office kitchen to gather some things and was met by Sarah McLachlan's song, "Angel" on a TV public service ad. I had heard the song before and was vaguely familiar with the lyrics, but this time it stopped me in my tracks: "In the arms of the angel, fly away from here . . . in the arms of the angel, may you find some comfort here."[12]

Once again, the combination of word and melody expressed the otherwise unspeakable pain and sorrow of the moment. I composed myself, grabbed what I needed, told my coworkers that I would likely not be back for the rest of the week, and left.

When I arrived at Rita's house, she was on the couch, propped up with pillows and wrapped in blankets, with Melissa and our family seated around her. She looked at each of us as though she didn't really understand what was going on or why all of us were there. I have since wondered whether her confusion may have been a blessing in disguise, perhaps a built-in defense mechanism, shielding her from the reality of impending death. The rest of us, though, were on our own.

Once Rita was in bed that night, our plan took shape. Each of us would take two-hour shifts sitting with her through the night while the others tried to sleep in one place or another. The presence of Rita and Melissa's two house cats, their two beloved dogs, and our Grace O'Malley added to the sense of the surreal. Despite the potential for chaos, they seemed to know that whatever was going on required them to be on their best behavior. Reet would have loved it. At one time, she had been a volunteer at the humane society and had to self-terminate her own visits there because she was prone to bringing home some of the furry clientele.

On Wednesday, Reet attempted to get out of bed, seemed to think better of it, and laid back down. She never got out of bed again. From that moment on, she gradually withdrew. Hospice had set up a morphine drip, which, for the most part, kept her comfortable, but on one occasion, I spoke directly in her ear and asked if she had any pain. Almost reflexively and without opening her eyes, she made a hand

---

12  Songwriters: Rudy Amado Perez / Sarah Ann McLachlan
Angel lyrics © Reservoir Media Music, Sony/atv Songs LLC, Tyde Music, Rubet Music Publishing Inc. 1997

gesture toward her abdomen. Melissa, following hospice instructions, increased the drip rate.

It was, to my knowledge, her last instance of communication with any of us.

By Friday morning, her breathing, which had been regular and rhythmic until that point, became labored. A hospice nurse visited and replenished the morphine supply. In the process, she commented that young patients like Rita (she was fifty-one) often had a strong will to live and would fight to the end. That fight was playing out before all of us, including my mother. The singular dread of every parent, the death of a child, was imminent. Her pain had to have been unbearable, yet she carried on, taking her two-hour shifts along with everyone else.

Midday, we received a visit from Father Joe Jacco, who had assumed pastorship of our parish just a few days before. He had been advised of Reet's condition and the relationship Rita and Melissa shared. A gentle, empathetic man, he listened more than he spoke, showing a personal interest in Rita's story. He ended his visit by administering the Last Rites of the Roman Catholic Church. It meant a lot to my mom that, in his kind and gracious words, a Catholic priest acknowledged the sanctity of the love that Rita and Melissa had shared over the past three years.

Rita's former partner, Ann, was one of many friends who came to say goodbye. Sometime around midday, Ann, Amy, and I went out to grab lunch. For the first time, Ann and I had a heart-to-heart in which she revealed that Rita wanted to "come out" to me and my family for a long time, but she, Ann, had resisted. Now, though, it hardly mattered. The woman with whom she had shared twenty years of her life would soon be taken from all of us. Our grief was very much her grief.

By early afternoon, Rita's breathing became more labored. All of us gathered around her bed, anticipating that every breath would be her last. My mom held one hand, Melissa the other. Mom would occasionally whisper to Reet that it was okay to let go. I know she felt that way, but Melissa wasn't ready. It would be yet another personal loss for her. She had already suffered the loss of her mother and two sisters. JoAnne and

I vowed to be supportive of this remarkable, resilient woman, yet we knew we could never replace the relationship Melissa and Rita shared.

At some point, Clancy and Baba Louie seemed to sense that it was time for them to say goodbye. They hopped onto the bed to offer comfort, sometimes laying across Rita or nuzzled next to her. Whether she was aware of their presence was doubtful, but she would have certainly approved even at the expense of increased discomfort.

True to the hospice nurse's words, Rita continued to fight, the determination we had all witnessed many times over the years coming to the fore once again. I had expected that she would have taken her last breath by this point, but still, she fought on. Rita was never comfortable as the center of attention. She certainly was that now, in a way she would have found very uncomfortable. When she was young, she would hide when it was time for parting at the end of family visits. Yet, five of us who loved her, plus three dogs and two cats, were there keeping vigil as the afternoon waned.

She had been such a life force for all of us. My thoughts took me back to the time she saw me pacing the hallway length on the transplant floor at Penn and, despite her pain and nausea, reacted with a look of pride and wonder. She had accompanied us on some of our Transplant Games adventures, always with a sense of awe at the joyous, living stories of donors and recipients. I believe she held deep satisfaction in my post-transplant athletic accomplishments and, even more so, in the wholeness with which I was able to approach my roles as husband and father, a wholeness that she had made possible.

I began to ask myself, *What would she want from me at this moment? What would she ask of the bearer of her life-giving organ as her own life ebbed?* She knew that for the last seventeen years, I had tried to make every day an expression of gratitude for the life she had given me. Was she telling me to act with the same defiance that characterized her courageous battle? If she was unable to confront adversity directly, perhaps I could be her surrogate. Maybe, in her last moments, she was willing me to celebrate her gift in the best way I could, in the one way that most clearly epitomized the spirit and vigor of the life she had given me. The answer began to come into focus: I would go for a run.

I changed into my running clothes, checked in with the others keeping vigil, told them what I was about to do, kissed Rita on the forehead, perhaps for the last time, and knew that I was doing what she would have wanted. Through eyes filled with tears, and with a lump in my throat, I headed out the door and broke into an easy jog.

The summer afternoon was warm but not humid or oppressive, and the sun was no longer at its most direct. The pace felt easy as my muscles gradually warmed up, allowing me to direct my thoughts to the present. I was, at that very moment, engaging in the one activity that, more than anything else, expressed the newness of a life I once almost lost and had never imagined regaining. I could feel Reet's indomitable spirit with me as though it was no longer confined by her cancer-ravaged body.

I turned on a side street and began a loop around Albright College in northeast Reading. With about one and a half miles behind me, I began to wind my way back in the direction of Rita and Melissa's house. About two blocks from their street, I saw our car pulling out. I knew that JoAnne was coming to look for me . . . and there could only be one reason why. She saw me, pulled over to the curb, and got out. Words were, once again, superfluous. My sister's long, spirited ordeal was over. Reet was in the arms of the angel.

I turned to face the late afternoon sun, fell to my knees, raised my arms to the sky, and shouted to the world, "Thanks, Reet! Thanks!" JoAnne and I embraced as I got to my feet. Then we gathered ourselves and got into the car for the short ride back to the house.

## POSTSCRIPT I

Early in the afternoon of September 6, 2007, two months to the day after Rita died, I received a call at work on my cell phone. It was Dave. Teresa had given birth to Sophie, a healthy seven-pound-three-ounce girl. The attending nurse's name was Rita.

## POSTSCRIPT II

It was a cold, gray Saturday morning in mid-January 2008. The Christmas decorations had been put away for another year. We had spent the holiday in Wilmington, our first Christmas as grandparents to three-and-a-half-month-old Sophie. Jim and my mom drove up from Florida to join us. It was my mother's first Christmas since losing Rita, and we were glad she and Jim decided to spend it with our family. Mom's health was beginning to fail, and within a few months, she would be on dialysis, but she was determined to meet her first great-granddaughter. Now, after the holiday hustle and bustle, all of us had returned to our homes and went about getting on with our lives.

JoAnne had gone out shopping, and I was running the vacuum. I had taken to streaming music from my computer to my hearing aids as a pleasant alternative to the noise of the vacuum cleaner. I chose a random play mode, ranging from classical to popular to Irish folk, with no control of the sequence of my selections.

I was leaning over while vacuuming beneath a table in our living room. As I straightened up, I found myself looking directly at a small, framed picture on the table. It had been taken at Giants Causeway during our Ireland trip and showed Rita, Melissa, JoAnne, and I shortly after we had encountered the shellicky bookey on the trail. At that precise instant, the Shellicky bookey song started to play through my hearing aids.

For a nanosecond, all reality was suspended, and time failed to exist. Then I let go of the vacuum handle, crumpled to the floor, and cried uncontrollably.

The odds of that particular song playing at that precise moment were infinitesimal. It had been over a year since the four of us sang that very same song on the cliffside trail to Giant's Causeway. Rita's presence was palpable. I had to believe she was telling me that all was well, maybe even that she approved of my music choices. When JoAnne came home half an hour later, I burst into tears again as I related the incident. She held me in her arms as I sobbed an exhausting flood of grief and gratitude.

## POSTSCRIPT III

On July 5, 2008, the day before we would observe the one-year anniversary of Rita's death, Dave, Teresa, JoAnne, and I drove to New York. JoAnne and Teresa had tickets to see *Mamma Mia!* on Broadway, while Dave and I planned to take in a Yankee versus Red Sox game at Yankee Stadium. Yanks/Sox in New York on a Saturday afternoon was the hottest ticket in town. Dave must have moved heaven and earth and paid a small fortune.

There was a certain familial symmetry to the occasion. Eighty years earlier, my grandfather first took my dad to "the Stadium" for a game. In 1954, my dad took me to see a game for the first time. Now, in the last year of the original Yankee Stadium (it was to be razed following the 2008 season, in favor of a new Yankee Stadium across the street), my son was taking me, putting a final punctuation on a four-generation

Gance family tradition. Yet, it looked like there might be a hitch in our plans. The day was overcast and rainy, and the forecast for the three o'clock start wasn't promising. The four of us grabbed lunch in Little Italy and, as we exited the restaurant, noticed St. Rita's Catholic Church across the street. We seemed to be drawn to it and found that the doors were open. We stepped inside. If we were going to see this game, we'd need all the help we could get.

A Catholic tradition holds that prayers can be offered through the intercession of a loved one, or anyone else for that matter, whom the petitioner deems might be in God's presence, God presumably being occupied with more weighty matters. Within the walls of St. Rita's, it seemed only fitting to see what Reet could do on behalf of Dave, myself, and 55,000 other Yankee and Red Sox fans hoping to worship at the shrine of Major League Baseball in just a few hours. For my part, I threw in a few prayers to my dad and grandfather just in case Reet hadn't yet acquired quite enough clout with the boss.

Our prayers dispatched, we walked out of St. Rita's and immediately saw that the rain had stopped and there were small patches of blue in the sky. While JoAnne and Teresa headed for Broadway, Dave and I got on the subway for the ride up to the Bronx. When we exited at the stadium, the sun was out, and areas of blue sky outnumbered clouds.

In a memorable game, the Yanks beat the Sox 2-1. Of the fans in attendance that day and those in the national television audience, only Dave and I knew that we had Reet to thank.

## EPILOGUE

Exactly twenty years to the day after my kidney transplant, close friends and family gathered at our home in Pennsylvania to celebrate Rita and the life with which she had gifted all of us. The day dawned bright, clear, and cold. Eight inches of fresh snow had fallen two days earlier. The light flooding through our windows called to mind the bright blue sky I viewed through my window on the transplant floor at Penn all those years earlier. Now, as then, the sparkling day was a metaphor for the wonder of the life I had been given.

Much had changed since Rita died on July 6, 2007. Sophie's birth to Teresa and Dave introduced JoAnne and me to the wondrous role of grandparents. The following summer, Amy married the love of her life, Zack Brown, a great guy from Georgia whom she had met during their concurrent stints as teachers in Mexico City. Rita would have relished both events and the rites of passage they represented in the lives of her beloved nephew and niece.

Amy and Zack flew up from Asheville, where they had settled, while Dave flew in from Wilmington, as did JoAnne's brother Kim and his wife Jeri. Kim and Jeri brought along a poster designed by one of their clever, artistic friends proclaiming "Gance Brand Kidneys" as the finest in filtering, secreting, and draining. It was signed by all present and is now displayed in our home. Fittingly, both Ann and Melissa joined us. Each had found themselves in new, loving relationships. Our celebration would not have been complete without them.

This would not be our first "Kidney Day" event. On major anniversaries such as the first, fifth, and tenth, we had invited Rita, Ann, and our friends to our home to celebrate with us. In the intervening years, JoAnne and I would take Rita out for dinner, sometimes joined by Ann and/or Amy and Dave. This, though, would be our first major Kidney Day celebration without the person who had made it all possible.

Many of our friends sang with us in the choir at St. Francis de Sales Church. It promised to be a musical feast, and it was. We were humbled and moved as the voices of those we loved rose in harmony in our home. Rita had been a music aficionado from the time she was young. She would have loved it.

Amy read from Ecclesiastes: "*To everything there is a season.*" It was not lost on anyone that Rita's season had been cut short—mine, by virtue of her selfless gift, extended. Dave read from Matthew 6: 25-34: "*I tell you, do not worry about your life.*"

Yet a celebration that was entirely solemn and reflective would not have been a true celebration of Rita. She had advised me prior to the transplant that her kidney liked at least one beer every day. I have gallantly endeavored to honor that. An Irish drinking song was called for. JoAnne and I selected "All for Me Grog," a fun and lively piece that seemed to fit. Reet's presence was once again palpable.

Toward the end of our gathering, our dear friend Bill Cambardella rose to announce that he had composed a song for me in memory of Rita. In addition to his role as music director at our church, Bill's music had been a part of the soundtrack of our lives for over thirty years. His voice graced the prelude at Reet and Melissa's commitment ceremony, he sang at Amy and Zack's wedding, and he had led our church choir at the celebration of life Masses for both Rita and my mother.

His song, "Another Chance," captured the overwhelming sense of gratitude that had guided my every thought and action since my transplant, as well as my determination to celebrate and cherish Rita's extraordinary gift. Today, we have Bill's evocative lyrics framed in our home. They continue to speak that poignant truth.

## ANOTHER CHANCE

Thanks to you, I see the sky.

I hear the wind; I feel her might.

I breathe deeply and raise my eyes.

My heart is beating, embracing life,

Grateful for another ride,

Another try, another hill to climb.

Thanks to you, I appreciate.

I savor each moment; I celebrate.

I enter the mystery; I am not afraid

To weep, to laugh, to love, to pray.

Grateful for another day,

Another way, another path to Grace.

We will dance!

Listen for the music.

We will dance!

When we use our strength, we don't lose it.

We will dance!

Finding courage in what few get:

Another chance to dance.

Thanks to you, we see her smile.

We hear her laughter and recognize

The flashing twinkle in your eyes.

The passion you bring to every inch of your life.

Grateful for the gift of time

With you, twenty years of brightly burning light.

The fullness of our hope:

To know and to be known.

We lead each other home

And we find joy when we let go.

## ACKNOWLEDGMENTS

Many friends and family had a hand in my writing this, and to the extent they did, it is a readable account of twenty blessed years that, at one time, I couldn't have ever imagined. As someone once observed, "You can't make this stuff up."

I'm grateful to Robin Mallernee, Dollie Llanso, Amanda Pace, Kathy Cochran, Mary Raine Moore, Linda Bair, James Greene, Sara Jenkins, and Sally Carlson for their helpful suggestions, and to Fred Morgan, Karen Dugas, Barbara Burke, and Ruth Perlmutter for their encouragement. Amy has reviewed it many times and was most helpful during my frequent wrestling bouts with Google Docs. Both she and Dave helped to refresh my memory about specific events, especially in the later parts of the story, and Dave's encyclopedic knowledge of matters dealing with *Calvin and Hobbes* was especially helpful.

Throughout the years, as my kidneys were failing and especially during the period when we were moving into our new home and I was starting dialysis, many friends carried us on their shoulders. They include Sue and Steve Horst, Scott and Judy Giacobbe, George and Mary Lou Michael, Bill and Michele Cambardella, Bonnie and Gerry Chasse, John and Barb Volpe, Victor and Jeaninne Kroninger, and Chuck and Betsy Corbett. Bill and Michele were especially helpful in providing me the encouragement to see this project through.

The doctors at Berks ENT Surgical Associates had promised me that when I needed to go for my kidney transplant, I would not miss a paycheck for whatever amount of time I needed. They were true to their word both for my transplant and during my rejection episode six months later. I've always appreciated their loyalty. My professional relationship with Dr. Franco Toso has been the most gratifying of my career, and I count him among my friends. To Dr. Winnie Kao, I owe the inspired suggestion to have my head shaved when Rita began chemo. Cindy Garrett, our office administrator, has been a dear and supportive friend for over thirty years.

A successful long-term organ transplant reflects the clinical excellence of dozens of doctors, nurses, dialysis nurses, and transplant coordinators along the way. To them, I owe my health and my thanks.

To the degree that this is a meaningful, cogent piece of work, I owe my endless gratitude to JoAnne, who also bears credit for the meaning in my life for fifty-five years. Her multiple reviews of my ramblings served to tighten up and focus these pages immensely. All throughout my slide into renal failure and the events that followed, she was at my side. I can't imagine going through this without her. It is, in many ways, her story too.

I hope that readers see that I have told my story in order to tell Rita's story. Hers is the story that begged to be told. Not a day goes by that I don't think of her, often wishing she was here to share an amusing anecdote. She especially enjoyed poking fun at some of the dumb things I would say or do. As much as anything, I miss being the butt of her one-liners. Her sense of humor was legendary. I imagine those of you who knew her would agree that she was completely selfless and without guile. She was a remarkable human being.

As I complete these pages, I have now carried Rita's kidney for thirty-five years.

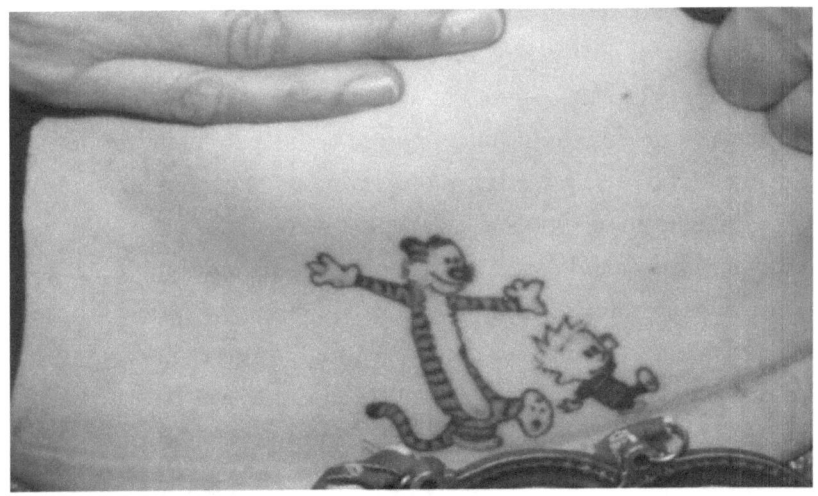
Rita's tattoo of Calvin and Hobbes traversing her nephrectomy scar

Bob Gance was born in Astoria, Queens, New York. He holds a doctorate in clinical audiology and held positions at a hospital and an ear, nose, and throat practice in southeastern Pennsylvania over a forty-year career. He is now retired and living in Asheville, North Carolina, with JoAnne, his wife of fifty-five years. They enjoy an active lifestyle together, thanks to his sister Rita's kidney.

www.ingramcontent.com/pod-product-compliance
Lightning Source LLC
LaVergne TN
LVHW041607070526
838199LV00052B/3017